FRANCHISING

The How-To Book

Lloyd T. Tarbutton

Prentice-Hall, Inc.
Englewood Cliffs, NJ

Prentice-Hall International, Inc., *London*
Prentice-Hall of Australia, Pty. Ltd., *Sydney*
Prentice-Hall Canada, Inc., *Toronto*
Prentice-Hall of India Private Ltd., *New Delhi*
Prentice-Hall of Japan, Inc., *Tokyo*
Prentice-Hall of Southeast Asia Pte. Ltd., *Singapore*
Whitehall Books, Ltd., Wellington, *New Zealand*
Editora Prentice-Hall do Brasil Ltda., *Rio de Janeiro*
Prentice-Hall Hispanoamericana, S.A., *Mexico*

© 1986 *by*

Lloyd T. Tarbutton

Englewood Cliffs, N.J.

This book is written to provide what is believed to be correct and authoritative information in regard to the subject covered. It is written and sold with the understanding that the author and the publisher are not rendering accounting, legal, or any other professional service. It is recommended that you consult competent professionals in specialized fields should you desire specific information.

Library of Congress Cataloging-in-Publication Data

Tarbutton, Lloyd T.
  Franchising : the how-to book.

  Includes index.
  1. Franchises (Retail trade) 2. Franchises (Retail
trade)—United States. I. Title.
HF5429.23.T37 1986   658.8′7   85-28188

ISBN 0-13-330143-5

ISBN 0-13-330135-4 {PBK}

Printed in the United States of America

Contents

DEDICATION x

AUTHOR'S NOTE x

ABOUT THE AUTHOR xi

INTRODUCTION xiii

CHAPTER 1: WHAT IS FRANCHISING? How to Figure Out Which
  Game to Play 1
  What Is a Traditional Franchise? 1
  What Should a Good Franchise Offer? 2
  What Are Business Format and Hybrid Franchises? 2

CHAPTER 2: IS FRANCHISING FOR YOU? How to Tell Whether
  Your Ideas Will Work 5
  How to Qualify Your Business 6

**CHAPTER 3: WHY DO COMPANIES GO INTO
  FRANCHISING?** How to Determine If You Should Sell
  Franchises or Develop Them Yourself 7
  Should You Go the All-Company-Owned Route? 8

CHAPTER 4: WHY DO FRANCHISES BUY FRANCHISES? How
  to Tap In on a Presold Marketplace 9
  How a Franchisee Can Choose Not to Fail 10

CHAPTER 5: WHAT IS THE FUTURE OF FRANCHISING? How
  to Look at the Past and Calculate Your Future 12
  Trends and Predictions for Franchising 13

**CHAPTER 6: IS THERE A NEED FOR WHAT YOU OFFER? Do
You Have to Have a Going Operation Before You Start to
Franchise? 14**
What Does "Need" Mean in the Marketplace? 15

**CHAPTER 7: DESIGNING YOUR OPERATION FOR
FRANCHISING How to Put Selling Creativity into Your
Business 16**
What Is Creativity? 17
Fourteen Elements of a Good Franchise 18
The Three Stages of a Franchising Company's Life 18

**CHAPTER 8: FOR EXPANSION: COMPANY-OWNED VS.
FRANCHISED UNITS, OR BOTH? How to Decide Where to
Grow 20**
How Does Available Capital Help to Chart Your Course? 20
Advantages of Having Company-Owned Operations 21
Key Advantages of Franchise-Owned Operations 22
Another Type of Franchising—Distributorships 23
How to Select the Right Regional Franchisees 23

**CHAPTER 9: WHY BUSINESSES FAIL How to Start and Stay in
Business 26**
How Experience Affects You 26
How Much Starting Capital Is Enough? 27
What You Need to Know About Record Keeping 28
Be Careful with Single-Line Sales 28
How to Learn Cautiously, Yet Wisely 29
Thirty Reasons Businesses Fail 30

**CHAPTER 10: THE CARE AND FEEDING OF YOUR BOARD OF
DIRECTORS How to Select Profit-Making Directors 32**
People You Should Not Choose 32
What About the President? 33
How to Select a Director 34
How to Train a Director 34
What to Pay a Director 36
How to Start a Director on the Right Track 36

**CHAPTER 11: LONG-RANGE PLANNING—48 HOURS How to
Make the Real Money 39**
How to Plan Your Work and Work Your Plan 40

How to Pick Your Planning Team   41
Benefits of the Plan   42
The Critical Steps in the Planning Process   42
Who Should Guide You in a Planning Process?   45
Key Forms to Get the Job Done   47

CHAPTER 12: SINK OR SWIM, BLACK OR WHITE, BELIEVE IT
      OR NOT   How to Put the Two Necessary Contracts Together   49
Your Franchise Contract   49
Which Contract Is Most Important   50
How to Go About Changing Contracts   50
How Important the Human Relations Contract Can Be   51

CHAPTER 13: DO YOU REALLY BELIEVE THE CUSTOMER IS
      KING?   53
Why Demographics Are Important   54

CHAPTER 14: HOW WILL A POTENTIAL FRANCHISEE
      EVALUATE YOUR FRANCHISE?   What You Should Put into
      Your Franchise System   55
Thirty-Four Things Potential Franchisees Look For   56

CHAPTER 15: CAN CONSULTANTS HELP AND ARE THEY
      WORTH IT?   The Fastest, Best, Least Expensive Way to Be
      Successful   58
What a Good Consultant Does   60
Checklist for Choosing a Consultant   61
What Do Consultants Charge?   63

CHAPTER 16: GETTING HELP WITH LAWS AND
      REGULATIONS   Important Names and Addresses in Franchise
      Law   66
How to Pick the Attorneys   66
The FTC Franchising Rule   67
How to Tell If You Are Involved in Franchising   68
Identifying States with Franchise and Business Opportunity
Laws   69

CHAPTER 17: TO JOIN OR NOT TO JOIN   Associations That Will
      Benefit You   77
How the International Franchise Association Can Help   77

CHAPTER 18: SYNDICATE, MERGE, SELL, GO PUBLIC, OR
        WHAT? Why You Need to Think About Structuring Your
        Company Now 79
    The Four Basics for Going Public or Selling Out 79

CHAPTER 19: LAYING OUT A FRANCHISE
        AGREEMENT Seventy-seven Things You Need to Consider for
        Your Franchise Contract 82
    Here Is Your Goal 82
    How to Project Twenty Years Ahead 83
    What Your Local Attorney Should Do 83
    When to Bring in the Franchise Legal Specialist 84
    Seventy-seven Items to Consider in Your Franchise Agreement 84

CHAPTER 20: ESTABLISHING FEES What They Are and How
        Much They Should Be 88
    Fees in Relation to Value 88
    How to Account for the Fees 89
    Considerations Regarding Area or Master Franchises 90

CHAPTER 21: QUALIFICATION AND SELECTION OF THE
        PROPER FRANCHISEES How to Select Franchises—a Critical
        Choice 91
    Why the Interviewer/Salesperson Is Important 91
    How to Build a Psychological Profile 93
    How to Screen the Potential Franchisee 93

CHAPTER 22: FRANCHISOR-FRANCHISEE RELATIONS How to
        Build a Strong Franchisee Organization 95
    How to Lose Franchisees 95
    How to Grow Franchisees 96
    How to Communicate with Franchisees 98
    How to Organize a Franchisee Association 98
    How to Write the Bylaws for Your Franchisee Association 100
    How Franchisors Should Participate 101
    Dos and Don'ts of Franchisee Associations 102

CHAPTER 23: EVERYTHING IS COMMUNICATION How to Get
        Things Done the Way You Want 103
    The Simple Elements of Communicating 105
    Watch Your Technical Language 106

Contents   vii

Why Never to Assume About Desires   107
How Never to Be Caught Off Guard   107
How to Teach Your Employees to Understand   107
How to Seek so You Can Find   109
How to Write and Speak to Get Action   110
The Importance of Feedback   111

CHAPTER 24: THE ARCHITECTURE AND DESIGN
    DEPARTMENT   Dos and Don'ts in Setting It Up   113
How to Know What to Believe   114
Change May or May Not Be Good   114

CHAPTER 25: THE FRANCHISE SALES DEPARTMENT   Here Is
    What You Need to Sell Franchises   116
Successful Sales Tools Used by Others   117
Should You Let Someone Else Sell Your Franchise?   119
What About Sales Territories?   120
Too Many Sales Can Put You Out of Business   121
Thirteen Items a Salesperson Needs in Order to Sell   122
Twenty-three Things a Potential Franchisee Wants to Know   123
Why You Should Get All the Buyers Together   124
Where to Get Sales Leads   124
How to Get Free Advertising and Free Leads   125

CHAPTER 26: THE SITE APPROVAL COMMITTEE   How to Get
    the Right Location   128
What You Need to Know About a Location   129
Computer Models for Selecting Locations   130
When to Use Real Estate Brokers   132
How to Pick a Good Broker or Salesperson   134

CHAPTER 27: THE TRAINING DEPARTMENT   Why and How You
    Should Invest Heavily in Training   137
Why You Should First Decide to Be a Y Company   137
How to Start Off Everyone Correctly   138
Please Do Not Cut Training Short!   139
How to Screen for Good People   141

CHAPTER 28: THE OPERATIONS DEPARTMENT   It Is Necessary
    to Control for Profits   143
How to Design Your Operations Manual   144

Developing a Field Inspector 144
How Much Is Enough Quality Control? 146

CHAPTER 29: THE ACCOUNTING DEPARTMENT Why You Need
    Good Numbers to Be a Money-Making Organization 148
How to Know What Decisions to Ask For 148
How to Establish Your Budget 149
How to Serve the Franchisee Uniformly 150
How to Cut Back on Paperwork 150
Computers and Manpower 152

CHAPTER 30: THE MARKETING DEPARTMENT How to Let This
    Department Take Over Your Company . . . And Make You
    Rich 154
The Only Business You're in Is the Marketing Business 154
How to Smell Out Free Stories 155
Your Public Relations Guide 156
How to Eliminate the Need to Sell 157
What About Advertising Agencies? 158
How to Be Creative 159
Ways to Work with Ad Agencies 160
Your Marketing Plan—Elements to Consider 162
How to Put Your Best Personal Face Forward 163
Staying on Top of Interviews and Speeches 165

CHAPTER 31: THE OTHER DEPARTMENTS As You Need Them,
    Be Ready to Add Them 169
Setting Up Departments 169

CHAPTER 32: LATER ON—EXPANSION Twenty Items to Consider
    for Down the Road 171
Thinking About Subfranchising 172

CHAPTER 33: CONSIDERING INTERNATIONAL
    MARKETS Knowing the Rules Is Number One for Success 174
Why You Should Never Assume Anything 175
How Small Companies Franchise 176
Why Companies Are Interested in Foreign Markets 177
Some Statistics on Foreign Growth 177
Foreign Franchise Associations 179

CHAPTER 34: THE IMPORTANCE OF AND HOW TO WORK
    WITH LEGISLATORS   Getting and Giving Legislative
    Assistance   180
Setting Up One Person for the Job   181
Some Useful Communications Tools   182
Who to Write to and What to Write   183
How and When to Use the Telegram, Mailgram, and Telephone   184

CHAPTER 35: THE QUALITIES OF A GENTLE TIGER   How to
    Pick Successful People   186
What Are the Desired Executive Qualifications?   187

CHAPTER 36: THE PHILOSOPHY OF WORKING WITH
    PEOPLE   Do These Things and You Will Suceed   191
My "Twenty-first Century" Management Techniques   192
Putting the Cash Register Ringers on Top   193
The Concrete Results   194
What's Better Than 100 Percent Results   197
How to Stem Employee Burnout   197
How to Deal with Different Ideas   198
How to Recognize What Is Not Said   200
How to Permit People to Feel Fulfilled   202
How to Decide Between Right and Wrong   203

CHAPTER 37: WHAT WILL BE YOUR DIRECTION NOW?   Would
    You Like to Learn How to Make Changes?   204
How to Approach Change   204

CHAPTER 38: GOVERNMENT FINANCIAL AND MANAGEMENT
    ASSISTANCE PROGRAMS   171 Names and Addresses to Help
    You   207
Minority Business Development Agency   207
Small Business Administration   214
Internal Revenue Service, Department of the Treasury   220

GLOSSARY   221

Dedication

To my many friends who rightfully share a large portion of the credit for this book. Over the years of learning experience they often walked in front of me, opening the pathway; behind me, pushing me onward; and yet always beside me with encouragement, advice, and friendship. They have assisted immeasurably in enhancing my educational process and my appreciation of franchising and life.

Author's Note

It always impresses me when someone who is supposed to be an expert shrugs his shoulders and admits he does not know the answer to all the questions. My confidence in him goes up immediately. When reading this book, it will be evident that I do not know all the answers. I do not say this to impress you, as I have mentioned above, but rather as a sincere caution.

Franchising comprises some forty different industries. Each industry is different. Within each industry are many, many companies which are also different. Each company chooses its particular method of doing business according to numerous factors. They may also be different because of experience, financial backing, personal desires—the list could go on and on.

If you multiply the various combinations of the foregoing variables, you will see that it is impossible to tailor a single book to fit all these situations exactly. On the other hand, there are basics that generally apply to most operations that select the franchise method of marketing. This is what I have endeavored to illustrate in this book.

About the Author

The International Franchise Association (IFA), headquartered in Washington, D.C., is the worldwide recognized spokesman for responsible franchising. The names of many of its members are household words, not only in the United States, but around the world. The individual franchise associations of numerous countries are affiliate members of IFA. One can rightfully assume that this association would not have asked Lloyd Tarbutton to write this book if they did not consider him qualified. Likewise, the IFA would not have become the sponsor of same.

Lloyd Tarbutton is a creative businessman—creative because he never accepts the idea "that's the way it has been done in the past" as valid for today. He teaches creative management techniques to business people from Norfolk, Virginia, to San Francisco, California; from Canada to South America; and from Europe to the Far East. He is co-founder of Econo Lodges of America, Inc., formerly known as Econo-Travel Motor Hotel Corporation, which introduced to the world an entirely new industry, the budget motel business. As the industry has evolved today, the application of the Econo System concepts can certainly credit them as being the founders. Lloyd Tarbutton started using the franchise concept of marketing when his company began, and it has continued to be a success. For a number of years, he served as president, CEO, and chairman of the board. For the last ten years, he served as chairman of the board, and is presently chairman of the board emeritus.

In addition, Mr. Tarbutton has served in various executive positions of the International Franchise Association, including that of president. He served on the board of directors, as a member of the executive committee, and as chairman of the past presidents advisory council. He was chairman of the first Far East International Symposium on Franchising held in Tokyo, Japan. Likewise, the first European International Symposium of

Franchising to be held by IFA was also chaired by Mr. Tarbutton in Amsterdam, Netherlands.

Mr. Tarbutton is an internationally known business consultant, specializing in the areas of franchising, self-motivating management, and creative sales and marketing techniques. He is chairman of the board of Tarbutton Associates, Inc. For over two decades, this firm has been active in commercial real estate development and management. Under its Hospitality Division, which is managed by his sons, hotels, motels, mobile-home parks, restaurants, and similar businesses are administered and operated.

He is a founder and served as vice chairman of the board of the Franchising Political Action Committee, Inc., which is headquartered in Washington, D.C. As chairman of the board, he served Rosemont Videotronics, Inc., a retail in-room movie distribution company; Econo-Travel Development Corporation; and numerous other companies. Mr. Tarbutton has been on the Norfolk board of the Bank of Virginia for many years. He is active as a trustee of the Old Dominion University Educational Foundation and is chairman of the board of the Center for Economic Education at the University.

While he holds numerous honorary titles, he is probably best known for his unique humor and practical approach to business, as an internationally recognized speaker at conventions, universities, and before civic organizations. He is a staunch advocate of capitalism and the free enterprise system. He was named to *Who's Who in American Business* when he was twenty-five years old.

To offer a unique balance, Mr. Tarbutton is also a franchisee. He is currently involved in seven different franchises that enable him to view the system from both sides, that of franchisor and franchisee.

The franchising system has needed a book like this for some time. The complexity of the subject is probably why someone has not written it before. This text is a work of experience rather than theory.

Introduction

The major part of me is fifty-two years old, yet there are other parts of me that have not been born yet (I hope)!

Often, a false sense of confidence develops with a little bit of knowledge. Here is a true example. I was privileged to hear a conversation several years ago between Mr. Smith and Mr. Jones. They were in different segments of the same industry. Both were using the franchising method of marketing. Mr. Smith had been in business for many years and had a large, successful company. Mr. Jones had been in business for only about five years but had made substantial progress. Since their businesses were closely allied in the same industry, Mr. Smith assumed he knew all about Mr. Jones's concept. He told Mr. Jones he had better give up his methods or one day he would wake up and find out he was broke. "One cannot make money in our business, the way you are trying to," he said.

I stood by and listened because I knew Mr. Jones had refined his concept uniquely and was prospering. He was considered a pioneer in his specialized field. Now, six years later, he is more successful than ever...in the same business. Mr. Smith's limited knowledge of his friend's concept resulted in dangerous advice.

Why am I telling you this? It is simply because you must be extremely careful about who you hire, who you listen to, and what you discern for your company. There are no simple solutions in the franchising business, only intelligent choices.

1

What Is Franchising?

How to Figure Out Which Game to Play

*Why didn't someone tell us what
kind of game we were playing or
how to play it before we started?*

The chain-store concept, which was the forerunner of franchising, dates back to 200 B.C. when a local businessman by the name of Lo Kass began operating several retail units in China. Perhaps the first could be earlier than that, when the first Chinese was assigned a specific route on which to operate his rickshaw. I am sure neither he nor anyone else guessed that business ventures around the world would later be assigning routes or territories that would eventually lead to franchising. Likewise, one can be sure, Louis XIV did not appreciate the groundwork he was laying when he granted countries to nobility and conditioned it upon them to pay him royalties that were collected from the population of those countries. Today's system of franchising still employs the original format of royalties. Many franchisors still grant franchising rights to entire countries.

WHAT IS A TRADITIONAL FRANCHISE?

Franchising as we know it today started around 1863 with the Singer Sewing Machine Company. Coca-Cola sold its first franchise in 1899. Next came the automobile and petroleum dealers, who decided to use the distributorship method of franchising in about 1910. They were soon joined by the soft-drink bottlers. These three became known as "traditional" types of franchisors, or were otherwise known as product and trade-name franchises. Primarily, they are product distribution arrangements.

The real growth of franchising was relatively slow until the 1950s and 1960s, when such terms as *franchising boom* and *franchise phenomenon* came into being. Since that time, a huge growth has taken place in what is known as business system or business format franchising.

The generally accepted definition for the term *franchise* is:

> A long-term, continuing business relationship wherein for a consideration, the franchisor grants to the franchisee a licensed right, subject to agreed-upon requirements and restrictions, to conduct business utilizing the trade and/or service marks of the franchisor and also provides to the franchisee advice and assistance in organizing, merchandising, and managing the business conducted pursuant to the licensee.

WHAT SHOULD A GOOD FRANCHISE OFFER?

The word *franchise* came originally from the French, meaning to be "free from servitude." In its present-day context, it means the same thing. You can avail yourself of the opportunity to own your business even if you lack experience and what would ordinarily be considered adequate capital. Thus, you are "free from servitude," your own boss. Ordinarily, if you were short on experience and capital, you would be crazy to think of going into a particular business. Not so if you consider a franchise.

This is true because, among other things, the franchisor will shepherd the franchisee with the benefit of experience. This assistance usually amounts to:

1. Site analysis
2. Lease or purchase assistance
3. Building design
4. Equipment layout and purchasing
5. Management training
6. Advertising and merchandising counseling
7. Standardization of procedures and operations
8. Centralized purchasing
9. Financial assistance/guidance
10. Use of presold national name
11. Continuation of all the above

WHAT ARE BUSINESS FORMAT AND HYBRID FRANCHISES?

When a franchisor offers all or part of the foregoing items with a fully integrated relationship, this is known as "business format franchising." It is typical of the newer types of franchising that range from fast-food restaurants and nonfood retailing to lodging, personal and business services, to rental and real estate services.

In addition to the traditional and the business format classes of franchising, there is also a third. It is known as a *hybrid* or *mixed* system. While it is most often referred to as "hybrid," I believe the word "mixed" describes it most accurately. It is just that—a combination of the other two.

From the foregoing, one can see quickly that franchising is not a business. Franchising is a method of doing business, a method of marketing a product or service to the public. Once you have a going business, it probably can be franchised. Franchising can be applied to almost any business. Let me show you, from a humorous standpoint, how true yet unlikely this statement could be. Here is a story that was related to me by Kenton Granger, a Kansas attorney.

UNUSUAL FRANCHISABLE INVESTMENT OPPORTUNITY

"I don't know if you would be interested in this," he wrote "but I thought I would mention it to you because it could be a real 'sleeper' in making a lot of money with very little investment.

A group of us are considering investing in a large cat ranch near Hermosillo, Mexico. It is our purpose to start rather small, with about one million cats. Each cat averages about twelve kittens each year; skins can be sold for about $0.20 for the white ones and up to $0.40 for the black. This will give us twelve million cat skins per year to sell, at an average price of around $0.32, making our revenues about $3 million a year. This really averages out to $10,000 a day—excluding Sundays and holidays.

A good Mexican cat man can skin about 50 cats per day at a wage of $3.15 a day. It will take only 663 men to operate the ranch, so the net profit would be over $3,200 per day.

Now, the cats would be fed exclusively on rats. Rats multiply four times as fast as cats. We would start a rat ranch adjacent to our cat ranch. If we start with a million rats, we will have four rats per cat each day. The rats will be fed on the carcasses of the cats that we skin. This will give each rat a quarter of a cat. You can see that this business is a clean operation—self-supporting and really automatic throughout. The cats will eat the rats and the rats will eat the cats and we will get the skins.

Eventually, it is my hope to cross the cats with snakes, and they will then skin themselves twice a year! This would save the labor costs of skinning, as well as giving me two skins for one cat.

Let me know if you are interested because I want only a limited number of investors. I think once we get the pilot operation going, we could franchise this business easily."

2

Is Franchising For You?

How to Tell Whether Your Ideas
Will Work

*I don't worry too much about what
is up ahead. I just go as far as I can
...from there I can see farther.*

To paraphrase a saying, "It used to be I couldn't spell the word *decision*. Now I are one." If you make a decision to go the franchising route, it needs to be totally part of you. As I see it, one can make that commitment only if one has reliable knowledge about the pros and cons of franchising.

What can you do? Reading this book is a start; hiring a qualified consultant is probably one of the safest bets; and you can also attend seminars put on by the International Franchise Association (IFA). There, you can learn in class and over coffee afterward from company representatives who are happy to swap ideas. They may not know much about your company, but certain problems are common to franchises. In addition, the general conversation is good, and very comforting.

You also could attend franchisor-sponsored trade shows, check out the published information from operating franchisors, and read what little there is in the library. There are a few magazines to which you may subscribe, but they mostly are geared to the sale of franchises, and to services or product information.

It may even help to stop by a franchised outlet and talk to a franchisee. However, if he had a problem getting supplies from his franchisor on Tuesday, you may get a very black outlook on the business.

As I mentioned earlier, be very cautious! Many good ideas have been dropped because of unqualified answers. Remember the Bible story of

5

how Samson slew thousands with the jawbone of an ass? Well, many good ideas have been killed with the same weapon.

Everyone likes to be an expert if you ask them for their opinion. They can tell you with great authority how to solve our problems with Russia, what would correct our oil-shortage situation, or why Mrs. Brown's children are such brats ... just ask them. I'm not saying don't ask; I'm saying that you need to qualify the "givor" before you agree to become the "givee."

HOW TO QUALIFY YOUR BUSINESS

Maybe you can be the best qualifier and confidante of all. Who knows more about your business than you do? No one, of course! Then ask yourself:

1. Is there a need for your type of business?
2. Does this need limit itself to an area or region?
3. Will this need continue to grow?
4. Have you been successful in your operations, using true and realistic accounting methods in determining profitability?
5. Can the inventory needs continue to be met on a uniform basis?
6. Would you pay someone $10,000 or $25,000 up front just for the right to have your business opportunity?

There are many more questions, but for the moment these are the most important. How did you do when acting as your own advisor?

Be careful of being so close to the forest that you cannot see the trees. Does your positive attitude stem from logical facts or does your heart delude you with romantic illusions of watching your own "business baby" grow up?

If you still feel good about the possibilities, you are probably ready to get some serious help. You may notice that I did not approach the question, "Is what you do suitable for the franchising business?" That is because franchising is not a business. Thus, almost every type of product, service, and so on is suitable for franchising if it has the capability of being profitable as a business.

It is okay to have doubts at this point. Francis Bacon in his *Advancement of Learning* said it well when he stated, "If a man will begin with certainties, he shall end in doubts; but if he will be content to begin with doubts, he shall end in certainties."

3

Why Do Companies Go into Franchising?

How to Determine If You Should Sell Franchises or Develop Them Yourself

Growth that adds dollar volume without improved methods is fat. Growth that dissipates existing methods is cancer.

"Sir, why are we standing in this line?"

"Well, because everyone else is standing in this line."

That is certainly not a valid reason either for standing in line or for going into franchising. There are, however, some very valid reasons why firms use franchise methods. The list could go on indefinitely if we considered all the possible personal motivations. I shall discuss the less emotional business reasons that seem to predominate.

Do you go the company-owned or the franchise route? You undoubtedly would prefer to own 1,000 company-owned units. It is usually true that company-owned units exceed the profitability of franchise units on the average. If you owned them all, you could have both ends of the stick.

However, this presents a problem. Everything in business has a price. Most companies do not have unlimited capital for investment. Thus, if expansion is the goal, if it is necessary to remain competitive, from a numbers standpoint, the franchise concept may be the solution.

By franchising, a majority of the risk capital for this expansion is put up by the franchisee. This is money you possibly could not get from conventional sources. It also takes a much larger staff to set up a company-owned and operational chain. By franchising, the market penetration can come about in a shorter period of time.

SHOULD YOU GO THE ALL-COMPANY-OWNED ROUTE?

Some business people do not go into franchising. They decide they are satisfied with their rate of growth, want only company-owned stores, and/or make a personal life-script decision for themselves.

Three years ago, I received a call from a restaurant owner who had a small chain of seven restaurants in another state. He hired me to look over his operation. He wanted me to tell him if he had a viable concept to franchise. I spent two days going over his business, seeing his home and life-style, and being around him as an individual. On the morning of the third day, he asked me if I had come to any conclusions about the viability of his concept. "Yes, I have. In addition, I have also discovered another question. Are you sure you are willing to change your life around and go to work again?" You see, he had arrived at financial security with his seven restaurants. His business was marketable as a franchise concept. Personally, I was not sure that he wanted to dig in on starting a franchisor company. As we sat there, we discussed what went into starting a franchise operation.

He concluded that he did not want to go into franchising. He was in his early fifties, had paid for his house and other investments, his children had gone through college, he had a general manager running all seven restaurants and an office, his other investments were paying off, and he just wanted to enjoy life more now. He had worked hard for many years. I detected this as he told me the proud story of how his business grew from nothing to seven restaurants. More money, expansion, market penetration... none of these were really of desire or interest to him now.

What are your desires for your company and yourself at this stage of life? There are many reasons why a firm begins to use the franchising concept of marketing. Most of them have to do with capital or market penetration. There are also reasons why they do not.

At this point, you may be thinking that this chapter has not given you enough to know whether to plan for the franchising method of marketing. You are right. Keep going. You will have to read almost the whole book before you can make that decision.

4

Why Do Franchisees Buy Franchises?

How to Tap In on a Presold Marketplace

People will buy almost anything. I know this guy in New York. His business is selling hang-ups. If you don't have any, you can buy one from him.

It has been said that the only certain things are death and taxes. Since going into business does not fall under the category of death or taxes, I guess success cannot be certain. The next best thing is to be as certain as possible.

There are a few other laws of the "I-told-you-so" society. For instance, there is Murphology, or Murphy's Laws, which have been well publicized over the years. They go something like this: If anything can go wrong, it will. Nothing is as easy as it looks. Everything takes longer than you think. If there is a possibility of several things going wrong, the one that will cause the most trouble will be the first one to go wrong. If you perceive there are four possible ways in which a procedure can go wrong, and you circumvent these, then the fifth way will immediately develop. If left to themselves, things will go from bad to worse. Captain Ed Murphy, a development engineer, is credited with starting these sayings, which today have become widespread.

We laugh at them, but in business we often wonder if they are not true. The public has heard and seen the problems that develop around them as they work for someone else. It is only natural that they desire as much security, certainty, and peace of mind as possible before going into business for themselves. Their logical thinking processes tell them to look for as much help and for the greatest percentages on the plus side as possible.

In walks Captain Franchise in all of his resplendent glory, with muscles rippling beneath his astro-colored costume, the fatherly look of caring and compassion upon his face, the tint of wisdom gray in his hair, and his hand outstretched for a handshake of comfort and understanding.

He obviously is successful; besides, Mr. Potential Franchisee has read and heard all of the press about Captain Franchise and his enormous success in the last twenty-five years. He then decides, "I want to go in with a winner. I want to go with Captain Franchise who will train me, guide me daily, and lend me his name, which is already known from 'shore to shining shore.'"

HOW A FRANCHISEE CAN CHOOSE NOT TO FAIL

Just what has the captain's press been saying that is so good? For one thing, it has been quoting success figures. I find that the numbers of successes and failures differ, depending on the government agency or association or publication to which one refers. In taking a correlation of these and interpolating as best I can, I find that you are much more assured of success when going into business if you choose to acquire a reputable franchise. The statistics for recent years show that if you go into business independently, without a franchise, the chances of failure during the first five years run around 65 percent. Should you choose a proven franchise, the chance of failure drops to about 2 percent to 4 percent. With odds so heavily chained toward success, you can easily see one reason why the franchising concept has enjoyed such growth.

The size of this concept is probably a little-known fact in the United States. According to the U.S. Department of Commerce, the franchisors and their franchisees account each year in dollar volume of sales for approximately one-third of all retail and service sales in the United States. At the present time, this is approximately $500 billion. There are approximately 500,000 outlets. In recent years, the annual dollar volume of business done by these outlets has generally been growing three times faster than our gross national product (GNP).

While the franchisee gives up certain elements of independence in running a business, he or she receives advantages for doing this. While some of these advantages are tangible, most may seem intangible. One of the benefits is the economic power of having the franchisor's name, the sharing of brand-name association. The franchisee also receives the transfer of management and technical expertise. In some cases, unique products and services are obtained from the franchisor.

In other words, the franchisor has charted the unknown seas, has weathered the storms, and has marked on the charts the safe harbors of profits and underlined in red the straits of business disaster. He or she has created a product/service that is presold, has established a reputation, and has unified a network of outlets with a centralized advertising pool for maximum benefits for all.

Due to experimentation, research, and a lot of money being spent, the potential franchisee can open a business with less capital than would generally be needed otherwise. His or her financing efforts probably will be guided by the franchisor, as will the business's design, decor, equipment layout, and so on. For these reasons, we can see why franchising is enjoying such growth.

5

What Is the Future of Franchising?

How to Look at the Past and Calculate Your Future

I have taken a large bite out of the apple of franchising. It is green... but sweet.

The future of franchising is... great! That one word is actually all you need for this chapter. However, you may find this statement easier to accept if you have a few facts to back it up.

Previously, I have given figures to sustain a pretty good case. Consider what has come about in your city. There is a cry for good services and products that meet specific needs at a fair price. As our society becomes more affluent, this cry will increase.

The U.S. Department of Commerce recently issued their latest edition of "Franchising in the Economy." It states that franchising has had phenomenal growth in the past, and continues to offer tremendous opportunities. In the last two years, the dollar growth of sales in relation to goods and services among franchising outlets increased 12 percent. The number of outlets increased by 17,954. It is estimated that employment in franchising went up more than 8 percent to over 5 million people. The number of companies who have joined the franchise system of distribution has grown about 6.5 percent annually for the last four years. These trends are expected to continue.

TRENDS AND PREDICTIONS FOR FRANCHISING

The rising complications of setting up business will account for a sizable portion of growth in the sale of franchises. In the years to come, there probably will be fewer independent businesses and more franchises issued because of oppressive government regulations and the high cost of operating.

Companies that are vertically integrated (only company-owned stores) and that have regional or national retail distribution outlets will be entering franchising because of cost factors, availability of capital, and the managerial advantages of entrepreneurial ownership. New and existing franchise systems will grow and new goods and services will be introduced.

The larger, more mature companies will increase their number of acquisitions and mergers among the existing franchisors and larger franchisee businesses. While this may result in fewer, larger franchisors, this will be more than offset by new companies entering franchising.

I see financially successful franchisors, while developing their distribution, continuing to grow in franchising. There is now new emphasis being placed on area or master franchising.

As much as it displeases me, I am afraid that government will continue to plague us with laws and regulations.

The future holds greater trends toward more scientific management, financial analysis by data processing, as well as cost and wage controls. The emphasis will be on productivity and profitability.

Due to the high cost of capital, more and more companies will turn to the franchising method of doing business as a means of expansion.

A complementary trend is taking place with the existing franchisees who know the advantage of their involvement with their franchisor. They will comprise a sizable portion of the growth in franchising as they become multiple owners/franchisees.

The U.S. Department of Commerce calls franchising "a significant part of the U.S. economy," and reports that franchising "continues to prove its validity as a marketing method adaptable to an ever widening array of industries and professions while providing immediate identity and recognition for prospective entrepreneurs joining the system."

Franchising, as a method of doing business, will keep on growing. In fact, stop right here and try to think of valid reasons why franchising would not grow. It is tough to do.

6

Is There a Need for What You Offer?

Do You Have to Have a Going Operation Before You Start to Franchise?

> *You can get much further with a kind word and a gun than you can with a kind word alone.*   Al Capone

For Al Capone, those words may have been correct. They are not of much value in a free enterprise system of economics. No one holds a gun to a customer's head and makes him buy from an appointed store. He who serves the customer's needs best gets the business.

There is a story about a large national manufacturer of dog food. The manufacturer was having its annual sales convention in Miami Beach, Florida. On the very first day, the president of the company got up before his 500 salesmen and proclaimed, "Surveys prove we have the best-looking dog food package on the market, we have the highest meat content of any on the market, our prices are under all our competition, our distribution is complete in every city and town. Why then, I ask you, are our sales down so low?" There was a short silence. Then a voice called out from the rear of the room, "The dogs don't like the taste of the darned stuff."

We can have everything going for us, but if the customers do not perceive a need in the marketplace, the franchising method of distribution cannot help you.

It is possible, as a franchisor, to start without ever having the first operation. It is possible—but generally not advisable. For one reason, legal registration and disclosures must state these facts. Likewise, sales are tougher for obvious reasons. You have nothing firsthand to show the prospective franchisee. Another important reason is, you had better know where the bugs are in your business before you sign a contract for multiple years with a franchisee owner.

There will be necessary refinements, changes, and physical improvements once you are operating on your own. This is also another way of proving need. Suppose your first operation does not do well or fails. This may not mean that your whole concept is bad. Perhaps it was just the location. There will be numerous other things you will want to do differently next time.

WHAT DOES "NEED" MEAN IN THE MARKETPLACE?

Need is a word that is somewhat misleading. The public may not need your product or service at all. They may, however, want it. As we use "need" in the business context, I mean "Will it sell?" Forget any other use of the word.

Need must, of necessity, take into consideration your capabilities. You may have invented the greatest widget ever known. If your capabilities for producing widgets are limited, you may need to consider alternate development plans. If you envision supply problems from manufacturers or distribution problems for certain areas of your desired market, this may prevent sales, even if a need does exist in that area.

I subscribe to the philosophy that there is always a way of solving a problem. I like one of Dr. Robert Schuller's sayings: "Problems are not stop signs, they are guidelines." I also endeavor to be a realist. If supplying a certain area at the present time puts you out of the local competitive price range, then we need to go back to the planning board. Note that I did not say "forget it."

Be careful of your own enthusiasm. When you develop a concept, product, or service, you undoubtedly feel that it is great. Since you have nursed this baby from birth, you acquire parental vision. Thus, you see only the good. This same type of thing happens with friends and respected business acquaintances. You ask their considered opinion. Their objectivity is probably restricted due to friendship or not realizing the depth of your question. If you have operating outlets, you are getting honest, objective answers from the public. The cash register either rings or it doesn't.

7

Designing Your Operation for Franchising

How to Put Selling Creativity into Your Business

The great empires of the future will be empires born of the creative mind.

"Realistic creativity" are two of the most important words in this entire book. To be realistic you must be extremely objective, concerned for facts that are reality; you must reject impractical and unsubstantiated visionary ideals. Both of these words seem to elude many new franchisors.

Setting up your company for franchising is not as simple as it appears at first glance. Let's say you have a marketable product, one that customers say is good. Okay, the product is good and you have a few company units going profitably, but now you have to create a whole new company (unofficially). You must now create an operation to market, sell, and service franchisee owners. This is a company within a company. The overall philosophy of the entire business structure needs to be worked out at this time.

Sure, you may be able to go along gradually and have things fall into place as you go, but it will cost you plenty during that time. In fact, it may cost your business. The very least damage one can sustain is probably growth that is only 50 percent of what it could have been. Now one can see the magnitude of this point.

WHAT IS CREATIVITY?

Back to that second word, *creativity*. Creativity is nothing more than rearranging the old in a new way. Let me give you an example. There are only twenty-six letters in our alphabet. Yet look at the thousands of books that have been written. There will be thousands on top of thousands created this year. They will be different and yet all created with those same old twenty-six letters everyone uses. The authors will merely be rearranging the old in a new way. That is creativity.

If the philosophy and physical structure of your company are like everyone else's, you will not become a best-seller. Call it marketing philosophy or whatever you like, this is a fact.

When we formed Econo Lodges of America, Inc. (formerly Econo-Travel-Motor Hotel Corp.), we did not invent one new machine, we did not bring into being one new service, and we did not design any new products. We rearranged what was already in existence, designed our concept around a new approach, and called it a "budget motel." The structure of the marketing, sales, and servicing of this approach were then tailored into forming the company.

Another example is Ray Kroc, the founder of McDonald's. He did not invent one single machine. He did not create a new sandwich. He did not design a new service. He rearranged all of the old into new ways with a marketing philosophy for his new restaurant. The great empires of the future are empires born of the creative mind.

Presuming that you have one or more company-owned operations, you will sooner or later ponder the question of expanding; in this instance, expanding by use of the franchising method. A few years ago, you almost could just say you wanted to start selling franchises and then begin. Today, it is a different situation. Anything that has become as successful as franchising is bound to have regulatory controls placed upon it. Franchising has arrived at that point. There are disclosure and other documents that must be filed with certain states and with every prospective franchisee. Your methods of operation and your track record must be covered completely in these documents. This is why your organization must be designed in advance rather than just being allowed to develop as the weeks roll by. DO NOT present a brochure or have any conversation with anyone in regard to the possible sale of your franchise until the legal requirements of disclosure have been complied with. The dollar penalties and, in some cases, prison terms for violation can be severe.

FOURTEEN ELEMENTS OF A GOOD FRANCHISE

Let us now look at a sampling of some of the other areas that must be pinned down when designing your franchise method of distribution. This list is not complete, but it will get you started in a thinking direction.

1. What are the detailed limitations on capital?
2. What marketplace will be targeted?
3. Establish profit centers within the organization with numbers assigned.
4. Decide the method of establishing the number of company-owned as well as franchised units.
5. Design all franchise owner services so as to be of visible value to those owners.
6. Establish a realistic evaluation of present corporate abilities.
7. Design a plan for filling the needs in reference to 6.
8. Design profit structures for present and ongoing franchise owners and your franchising company.
9. Design operational policy for quality control.
10. Design all fee and income source structures.
11. Set up reasonable goals in all areas.
12. Detail design and equipment layouts.
13. Design the training program.
14. Design all sales, marketing, operational, etc., tools.

The list goes on and on. From time to time these items will change. However, the more you can pin down with "experience accuracy," the faster and more profitable you will grow.

THE THREE STAGES OF A FRANCHISING COMPANY'S LIFE

In a realistic, growing franchising company, there are three basic stages. The first is the entrepreneur stage. The founder, trail-blazer type, is everything to everyone. He heads up marketing, sales, operations, every department. As years go by and a company becomes more successful, the professional stage begins. In this stage, the founder steps (or is pushed) aside for trained management to run things. Last comes the philanthropic stage. This occurs when the profitability and size of the company reach such proportions that the owners feel inclined to contribute to the needs of society.

I'm sure that all franchisees want to reach the third stage as fast as possible. If that is to happen, you must plan carefully. If you fail to plan, you are often planning to fail, or at least planning not to be as successful as you could have been. Yet planning in an area where you have no previous experience is very difficult to do. This is why acquiring assistance from someone else is usually necessary. It is the "chicken or the egg" problem. How do you detail plans for your company's growth if you have not been in franchising and done these things before? Yet these things have to be done before you plunge in, if for no other reason than the fact that you must describe them in the legal disclosure documents. The least expensive route toward the fastest profit is to get help. That help may come from inside or from outside of your organization. I will talk more about this in Chapter 16.

Regardless of how you do it, designing your operation to become a franchising company is a crucial step in your development. It can mean a difference of years in terms of progress.

8

For Expansion: Company-Owned vs. Franchised Units, or Both?

How to Decide Where to Grow

You have removed most of the road-blocks to success when you have learned the difference between movement and direction.

When starting to franchise, most companies make a general decision with regard to new units. That philosophy often winds up to be: "Put together the deal however, wherever, and with whomever you can." In other words, there is a decision, but there is no exact direction.

It is tough to turn down a possible deal, but if it does not fit in with your "plan," you are time, money, and manpower ahead to let it go by. Throughout every phase of your operation, there should be a firm plan of action to follow. It will bring results more pleasing than anything else you can do.

HOW DOES AVAILABLE CAPITAL HELP TO CHART YOUR COURSE?

In planning for franchised or company-owned units, or both, the available capital is probably one of your first considerations. The type of business you are in has significant bearing in this area. If you are in the motel business, your capital requirements to establish a new unit are much larger than if you are in the quick-copy printing business. In the motel business, you need land, a specialized building, furniture, and equipment—all of which have large dollar price tags. In the quick-copy business, you can probably lease a store-front office/shop as well as the equipment. The advance deposits on the leases probably would be only $2,000 to $3,000.

The various methods of obtaining capital and financing differs according to the type of business you are in. This is a huge area that can spread from syndications to leasebacks and standard mortgaging. I will not attempt to cover these here. Financing and capitalization, however, must be worked into your plan for yourself and your franchisees. Your available capital and financing will definitely influence the emphasis you place on opening company-owned units versus franchised units.

With company-owned units, you have complete management power. It is absentee ownership, but I assume that your controls are satisfactory to handle this. If not, they must be or it will cost you.

ADVANTAGES OF HAVING COMPANY-OWNED OPERATIONS

One of the plus items for company ownership is the fact that you earn the total profits from the units. Your growth pattern in a city or region can be according to a master plan. Your feedback from the units will assist you in quality controls and overall system improvements. Adherence to company standards will be more exacting. There are also legal advantages in company-owned units. Advertising cooperation on local levels is less expensive per unit. If the company units are clustered in geographic areas, local management can develop greater market potential faster.

Company-owned units allow for more flexibility toward changing strategies in all phases of the business. Company regional people will often be the trend setters for the franchised units. They do this with their personal direction as well as the influence of experimentation and change. Thus, statistical data may be obtained quickly in company units. This is definitely more accurate and therefore more dependable for quicker decison making.

On the other hand, most of us do not have unlimited funds with which to open all company units as fast as we would like. Perhaps there is also a manpower problem. Maybe penetration of the market is a necessity in order to maintain a leadership role. Wide geographic coverage might be another problem. We may not want to place additional liabilities or contingent liabilities on the company's financial statements by going the company-owned route. All of this brings us to the possibility of franchisee expansion.

KEY ADVANTAGES OF FRANCHISE-OWNED OPERATIONS

It is probably a fact that the best fertilizer for a business of any kind is the owner's foot on the premises. With a franchise, the franchisee-owner is usually there or closely allied with the unit operation. The owner is or can become more of a part of the immediate community, which builds acceptance for his unit. Local knowledge of the market can build sales and prevent or reduce costly errors.

The motivation of the on-the-spot owner is usually translated into the possibility of lower unit costs, free extra hours of his personal labor, and faster decisions for local condition changes. Naturally, there are exceptions to all of the above; however, we are dealing in generally accepted principles. In some businesses, the company-owned units will outperform franchisee operations.

Through franchising, you may be able to create a larger niche in the marketplace faster than with company-owned development. The franchisee owners themselves may become multiple owners or will certainly radiate other sales of franchises. The fees and royalties they generate will naturally add to your profits. There are costs involved with a franchise operation that you would not have if all were company-owned. These costs must be weighed when considering which way to go.

One thing for sure, it probably costs as much (or nearly so) to service thirty franchisee-owners as it does to service sixty. For every franchisor business there is the law of diminishing costs and a break-even point. Once you cross that break-even point, the numbers can show extremely beneficial improvements, especially if you are tuned to cost-center controls. If not, you may still show profits but you will not realize their full potential as quickly.

With all factors considered, you may decide to go with a combination of company-owned and franchised units. What is the right mix? I cannot give you a generalized answer on this. It is tied too closely to your personal operation. The decision must come from exact facts, circumstances, and personal company objectives.

ANOTHER TYPE OF FRANCHISING—DISTRIBUTORSHIPS

There is another type of franchising which should be touched upon here, and that is *distributorships* and/or *area franchises*. If you are in business as a manufacturer or are considering area franchising, the concerns will be somewhat similar.

You may be a manufacturer distributing to regional or area wholesale distributors or you may distribute directly to the retail outlets. Let us consider distribution to a regional wholesaler who has rights granted for your product or service.

Finding this type of potential franchisee is a special project. He must have sufficient financial muscle and be willing to develop an adequate market area. He must start with a staff organization of qualified people to carry out the undertaking.

HOW TO SELECT THE RIGHT REGIONAL FRANCHISEES

The choosing of the regional franchisee is specific, and must be done with greater care than any other. In addition to the reasons outlined above, this is merely a good business requirement. Suppose you have a region where fifty retail outlets could be established. If one turns out to be a franchisee owner who is hard to work with, undercapitalized, misleading on his application to you, or is simply not interested in expansion to any greater extent, you have a problem. However, this one retail outlet out of fifty is no great loss when you average him in with the region. On the other hand, if you get a regional distributor who has some or all of these problems, it probably will affect the entire region, or all fifty retail outlets.

Since it is so vital for your entire region, check out the psychological makeup of your potential franchisee distributor. Focus on his desires as well as his capabilities. Will he put forth the financial strength to develop his market with advertising, sale promotions, warehousing proper inventory, financing receivables, meeting payrolls, and then expansions? Will he gear his sales and services of general operation for continual growth?

Contracts are good but a clear understanding is equally valuable. Do you and he understand the mutual obligations and their limitations? Will he agree with and abide by the tested marketing methods you suggest? Is he willing to become totally familiar with your product, policies, and procedures in order to thoroughly avail himself of all opportunities?

It is also important to find out whether your objectives are in conflict. That may sound strange, but the primary objective of your manufacturing management is probably to increase sales volume on all of your manufactured items that are marketable in the regional distributor's area, while the distributor's primary objective may be to increase his profitability or his return on capital invested in his distributorship. This objective can be increased by either increasing sales, which you as the manufacturer would like, or by a larger spread on the distributor's cost-sales price profit.

The distributor may not find it most advantageous to increase sales volume because it will take additional capital expenditures for warehousing, product sales, and financing of additional receivables. He may be able to increase the profit spread, yet maintain the same volume of business, by raising the sales price on your products. He may even be able to decrease the product cost without increasing sales volume and assist his profits. Perhaps he will take your most profitable items and concentrate only on them. This also may raise his profits without increasing total sales and actually lower his costs. All of these conflict with your objectives to some extent.

Since many distributorships are multiline, there may be another conflict. The promotion of one line may be in direct competition with your product. More than likely the distributor will carry noncompeting lines which complement yours. Indirectly, though, they are competing. They compete because the distributor probably has limited capital resources, limited sales representative time, and perhaps limited display and marketing spaces.

Complacency is another area where one should be alert. It can be a problem on either side and can mess up a relationship in almost any direction. The manufacturer who was hungry in the past but is fat today may not listen as closely to his individual distributors when they call for expanded programs, better long-range planning, and more profitable products in order to meet competition and/or expansion. The distributor may be satisfied to continue a natural 7 percent growth rather than take an aggressive attitude for 20 percent. Both, because of complacency, may fail to live up to potential or agreements that may be brought about by short-lived periods of success.

The ideal for both manufacturer and distributor would be for the manufacturer to provide the products, programs, and price structure to allow the distributor to compete successfully in his region and chalk up a good rate of return on his investment.

The distributor should obligate himself to the necessary financing, manpower, and attention to business in order to acquire a rate of growth and penetration that is acceptable to both parties.

If these qualities are the goals of the potential franchisee distributor, you have the right person for your expansion program.

Even if you are not a manufacturer or a distributor franchisor, you might like to read over this section on distributorships again. The same criteria and problems generally will apply to regular individual unit franchisee owners.

9

Why Businesses Fail

How to Start and Stay in Business

*Those who forget the lessons of the
past are doomed to relive it.*

It is truly a wise person who learns from the mistakes of others. After all, no one lives long enough to make them all himself. Likewise, few have the financial resources to be able to fund constant, serious mistakes.

With this in mind, we might look at why businesses have failed in the past in an effort to guide us in our future endeavors. Each industry will have a list of different reasons when analyzing those who failed. Generally, no matter what your type of business, there will be two items that appear consistently. They are lack of actual experience in the various phases of the business one is starting and/or lack of adequate capital.

HOW EXPERIENCE AFFECTS YOU

First, let me give you an idea about what lack of experience could have done, even to a company that was already established. I remember a few years back, when the budget motel industry was only about four or five years old. At that time I was chairman of the board, CEO, and president of our company. The duties of those offices were just too much, so I decided I would seek someone to become president. A committee of board members was formed for this project. After careful planning, qualifications were drawn up for a president. The word went out to the motel and hotel industry. We located the two largest motel/hotel executive recruitment firms in New York. A large group of applicants was screened down to fifty people. That is a sizable number to have it made it through our qualifications. We took the files on each of those people, weeded them to the top twenty, and set up personal interviews.

When the last interviews were finished, the committee agreed that none were acceptable. Most of those interviewed were excellent and capable hotel/motel executives with good histories. What was the problem? They had no experience in the exact field we were in—the "budget" hotel/motel business.

After the second or third interview a realization began to form. The applicants needed experience in the executive areas of a "budget" hotel/motel chain as well as in a franchising company. Several had those qualifications, but not in the budget business. We decided to be safe and grow a president in house.

Now, years later, with additional knowledge and twenty-twenty hindsight, was that a good decision? Yes, it was. You may be a top executive, but if you do not have complete experience in the various technical departments, either get it or hire it if you want to be assured of as much success as possible. This may not be as important in a giant departmentalized corporation. There you have experienced executives below you who probably run departments as large as your company.

HOW MUCH STARTING CAPITAL IS ENOUGH?

Next let us discuss lack of adequate capital. I guess it is rare for any new company to have as much as they would like. If you do, you still have to be concerned with the return on assets (ROA) or return on equity (ROE). How much is enough? That depends on your plan of action. How do you get a plan going so you can tell how much is enough? The plan depends on your reasonable possibilities with reference to capital, marketplace need, competition, and so on. So now are we to the "chicken or the egg" stage? Not exactly.

At some point we begin to form an idea plan, using chiefly experience from the past. Consult with someone who has done it before, someone who has started a franchising operation and can offer mileposts from which to figure. After these various bases are calculated, a price tag will develop.

Total up the figures. Then develop a backup plan in case it takes more money (and it usually will). You need a plan whereby you can fall back and still have a cash cushion for contingencies. No good general ever goes into action without an alternate plan. In fact, he probably has two or three of them prepared, depending on which way the campaign moves.

I have seen many businesses come so close to making it, then, because of various circumstances, cash becomes tight and they have to fold or sell out. The buyer then carries the business by feeding in the required cash to keep it afloat for six or eight months more. Gradually he comes out of the red and starts climbing into the black, only to have a great success.

WHAT YOU NEED TO KNOW ABOUT RECORD KEEPING

There are other reasons why some businesses fail. Any one or a combination of them could possibly bring down a good idea. Take record keeping, for instance. In today's sophisticated business world we must keep timely records. If you are the entrepreneur sales type, you probably already have a dislike for paperwork. Look out, because it can get you. If you let it go, you could lose your business or, at the very least, additional money.

Tied in with the record keeping come statistics, trends and cost analysis ... all in the paperwork area. I know a businessman who always kept his bills and checkbook in his car trunk. Once or twice a year he would make a stab at getting organized. If there was a good checkbook balance, things were going great! I've known him for years and thought that one day, if things got tight, he would go under. Sure enough, it happened. You need to know cash flow by the season of the year, have a cost analysis on your product or service, have trends graphed out, be familiar with retail pricing structures, and all the other thousand and one details in order to be on top of your business.

If cost centers are not maintained, the little leaks of red ink may bring you down. Those small problem spots can create real trouble if left untended. Watch all of your business. Make every area a center of control.

BE CAREFUL WITH SINGLE-LINE SALES

Single-line sales and single-line thinking can also be causes of failure. Note how many items are now on the McDonald's menu boards. For a number of years they were practically a single-line operation ... hamburgers. As competition and conditions changed, they stopped thinking in one line. They experimented and now, twenty-five years later, still run a profitable business. Where do you think they would be if they still were single lined with one type of hamburger, french fries, and drinks, as they did for the first ten years? That's right—probably out of business or certainly going downward.

This single-line thinking usually means ignoring the signs of new developments. This could occur in the technical side of manufacturing or all the way to new developments in connection with your competition. Doing things the same old way in a fast economic climate of competition and change usually means going backward. Be aware, be open, and above all allow creativity to flourish.

HOW TO LEARN CAUTIOUSLY, YET WISELY

Failure or slowed growth often comes to one who is his own expert. You are probably familiar with the saying attorneys have, "He who acts as his own lawyer has a fool for a client." This has some real applications in business. Evaluate realistically your areas of expertise. More often than not, trying to save a few dollars on professional assistance or advice is very expensive. Knowing what not to do is often as important as knowing what to do. You may not fail, but the slowing of possible growth can be very real. The sad part about this point is that you usually will never know or possibly ever question what could have been.

I have learned much from competitors. What has happened to them helps me make better decisions. This is fondly referred to as "going to school on someone else." Learning from others is one of life's most valuable lessons. Ignoring our competitors' mistakes is another reason for business failure.

Some businesses fail because of political infighting. Jealousies, partnership inequities, and the "let everyone shift for himself" attitude can all cause trouble. When people who work together are busy trying to outsmart each other rather than concentrating those efforts toward a single company effort, difficulties will usually emerge.

Success can sometimes bring about the failure of a company. This statement may sound crazy, but a company that begins to enjoy success will often expand beyond its capabilities to manage or finance. The talent of management and finance must be on sound footing in order to consolidate size and success. One must program and control growth. Growth that adds sales or production volume without improving methods is fat. Growth that curtails productivity or sales is a cancer.

Let us look at failure by nepotism. Family empires have been a factor in every country in every age. It may be an attractive way to keep control, but watch out. The problem is not just cash drain going out to a son-in-law. Ineptness is often overlooked because of lack of awareness, not to mention how difficult it is to come down hard on a relative.

Another factor is morale. Your staff can be demoralized when it becomes obvious that the family is getting the top management positions. Imagine yourself in that situation. What happens to your morale when you as a conscientious, eager, qualified management candidate find the ladder to the top blocked by family members? This could cause your company to lose important people. I am not saying nepotism is always bad. In certain circumstances it may fill deserving needs. Just be aware of the possible problems.

Recently, an astute businesswoman made a very intelligent observation. She said, "I have had a lot of success with failure." She went on to explain she had learned a lot from her failures and the failures of others. Success has come to her from those learning experiences. This is a very wise person.

THIRTY REASONS BUSINESSES FAIL

Here are some other pitfalls which cause businesses to fail. Since most of them are self-explanatory, I will just list them.

1. Insufficient control over the cost and quality of your product
2. Lack of proper stock control
3. Buying short or selling long
4. Underpricing the goods you are selling (often due to lack of knowledge of actual cost)
5. Poor customer relations
6. Failure to promote and continue promotion of your public image
7. Poor public relations with suppliers of goods and services to your company
8. Management's lack of ability to reach decisions quickly and act on them
9. Failure to keep pace with management aids as conditions change
10. Real and psychosomatic illnesses of key people
11. Reluctance to be aware and seek professional assistance when needed
12. Failure to minimize taxation through proper advice on tax planning
13. Inadequate insurance programs
14. Lack of planning and forward impetus in sales department
15. Poor human relations with your staff

16. Loss of key personnel
17. Lack of total knowledge of product, merchandise, or services that are performed
18. Inability to foresee and cope adequately with competition
19. Complacency about competition
20. Failure to anticipate market trends in connection with the products or services you sell
21. Failure to anticipate market trends with regard to purchases
22. Lack of control of liquid assets
23. Insufficient planning for future capital needs
24. Failure to stay within the bounds dictated by capital availability
25. Lack of budgeting or failure to acknowledge and follow same
26. Refusing to recognize factuality of financial position
27. Poor record keeping
28. Granting of too much credit
29. Purchasing too much on credit
30. Poor receivables control

As we view why businesses fail, we often see visions from the past. Those who forget the lessons of that past are possibly doomed to relive it.

10

The Care and Feeding of Your Board of Directors

How to Select Profit-Making Directors

*If I have seen further than others, it
is because I have had the privilege of
standing on the shoulders of giants.*

If you are in business for fun, then go ahead and play games. If you are in business for such reasons as personal development and satisfaction, business growth, making money, serving the needs of others, and similar worthwhile goals, then choose your top leadership wisely.

If you are in it for fun, stacking the board of directors with family, close friends, your executive officers, and the like may be just right—you will have a good time with a group that will vote the way you want. For maximum company progress, I doubt seriously that they would be the ones you should choose. I am not saying family, friends, and so on are not smart. I am saying, define your purpose, then choose your people.

PEOPLE YOU SHOULD NOT CHOOSE

James A. Mather, founder and chairman of the board of the Mr. Steak chain of restaurants, once gave me some good advice. "If you want the best guidance for your company, choose people who are not subordinate to your position or your personality."

Imagine this situation. The president and his officers are the directors. As a director, each of the officers is in the position of being the boss of the president. Can you imagine those directors criticizing the president or his management policies when they work for him all but that one day per month when they have a board meeting? That president has the power to make their life miserable and even to fire them.

This is not a problem if you have fully actualized people with their psyches in the right place, who understand the meaning of self-worth. They have the "I'm okay, you're okay" feeling in their possession. Do you know many people who have life this well put together? Do you know any board that has these qualities?

Now, back to the situation. If you are an active chairman, the same problem related above applies to you. Few on that board are going to let you have it between the eyes for any bad policy you may foster. This dilemma can go on and on. If you have your CPA, attorney, supplier, family member, anyone who has ties with you or the company on that board, they walk a dual line—a line you can cut at any time. You will not get the best of their brains in board meetings. Human nature has to put self-preservation above loyalty to the stated purpose of directors according to your corporate charter and bylaws.

If you are starting a new business there may be no problem. You can choose wisely the nominations for directorship. If you are already constituted, it is probably another story. Corporate policies of who owns how much stock may be a factor. Assuming that good common sense will prevail, lay it on the line and ask for resignations so the board may be reconstituted.

WHAT ABOUT THE PRESIDENT?

You probably will want to retain the president of the company on the board. In fact, your bylaws or state law may make that mandatory. Choose members of your board for the qualities of brainpower, expertise, and freedom to say what they think. People who hold earned positions in their fields are not likely to be intimidated by you or your company. Now you are getting the best of the brainpower of the best.

When you have board meetings and need a report from one of the department heads or officers, schedule it. Have him come in, make his report, answer questions, and leave. This does not allow that officer to be privy to the pros and cons of various board members. The president may disagree with the item discussed, but if the majority of the board votes it, he should effectively carry it out. He must do this with enthusiasm. As far as his officers are concerned, it was a unanimous decision. They do not pick sides, even subconsciously. The spirit of the company is preserved on the positive side.

HOW TO SELECT A DIRECTOR

I guess the next question is how to go about picking a director. Because someone is eminently qualified in his field does not mean he is right for your board. He or she may be great as the head of the community fund, tops as a heart surgeon, or even the greatest sales motivator around. As one who participates in planning the overall goals of your company, that may be another story.

Symbolic boards also can be deceptive. The boards of the church, the hospital, the build-our-city-better organization sometimes are serving because they are willing workers for the purpose of that association. If someone serves on a college board, it may mean he has the ability to raise money or to contribute directly. Agreeably, these often are people who have great, self-made success stories behind them. They may be good for your board, but consider all the facts and then decide.

After deciding who you want, be sure the candidate understands what you expect before you allow him or her to accept. Lay out a detailed description of a board member's duties. Put in the boiler-plate explanation that is in your bylaws and the laws of your state, then put in the down-to-earth, easy-to-understand words that spell out how you go about performing all those polysyllabic legal phrases the law requires. Explain what training and educational process you expect so he or she can understand the workings of your company. This will allow the candidate to make more intelligent decisions in that board meeting. The laws generally say that a director must perform "due diligence" in learning about things on which he or she is expected to make decisions.

HOW TO TRAIN A DIRECTOR

Being a board member is something one is trained for. It is not an inherited ability just because one is a good business or professional person. Training in the decision-making process as well as in the technical side of your business and the normal processes of budgeting, goal setting, and management policies is necessary. You must school the board members in the amount of free flow you allow in your meeting. A good potential board member will question you in advance on all these things if you do not offer him or her this information.

Some people will not sit on a board as a figurehead. The possible exception is a board that serves a community or philanthropic need. I for one am not interested in being a puppet to feed someone else's ego needs. If I cannot contribute honestly, I will not serve.

Much can be wasted by petty situations that go on and on. An example of this is a board in Canada on which I was asked to serve. I looked into the situation and agreed. At my very first meeting, after about forty-five minutes I detected two factions in the room. This told me either the goals were not uniformly laid out or people were not communicating honestly. In either case, time and benefits to the company were being wasted. Since I was the new kid on the block, I tried nicely to cut through the polite rhetoric and find out what was the score. This did not work. I decided it was time for a speech.

"Gentlemen, I detect we are playing boardroom games. There are obviously two sides here, and I do not know what is going on. I cannot contribute to the decision or vote in the dark. Will someone please enlighten me?"

There was silence. Finally, one man spoke: "Okay, if X and Y will leave the room for a few minutes, I'll explain what has happened."

I was shocked! Leave the room? Were these grown-ups or children? That did it. "Gentlemen, I did not come a thousand miles and take two days of my time not to be honest with you. I hope you feel the same. If there is someone in this meeting who needs to be called a jerk, then let's do it, explain why, allow him to answer, and then we can intelligently decide accordingly. If we do not, this illusory conversation I am hearing could go on for many monthly board meetings and accomplish nothing. In fact, it would probably hurt the company by lack of decisive actions. If this is the case, it will be without me. I am only interested in short, direct, straight talk."

There was a long silence, during which the chairman did not make a move. A member finally broke the silence. He began by saying that he felt I was right and that he had a bone to pick with one member about the way a deal was handled for the company. He went on for twenty minutes. He was to the point. When he concluded, the accused man got up, went to the speaker telephone on the table, and said, "You are incorrect. The one person who can explain this situation is Mr. M. If you will allow me, I will call him on the speaker phone. I will ask him directly and you can all hear his answers." They agreed; he proceeded to do so; Mr. M. answered; the accuser was wrong; he apologized; the point was made.

At the end of the board meeting I asked how long the subject had been boiling. The accuser said that he had heard the rumor four months prior and he guessed eight to twelve hours of little group meetings among three of them had taken place.

Let us say it was ten hours with three people. That is thirty man-hours plus all the individual priority thinking time the situation had taken in between. It could all have been eliminated if they had not been involved in board games and dishonest communications. Directors need to be trained.

WHAT TO PAY A DIRECTOR

Pay your directors more than you think they could possibly be worth. Good people will pay you back many times in creative, astute management guidance. These are the people who will be directing the very life of your company. Their decisions are critical to profits and, above all, losses. I know pay is possibly a problem if your capitalization is thin and you are just starting. There are different ways of being worthwhile to directors; perhaps future benefits can be attractive.

Boardmanship is partially a learned skill. Part of that skill lies in the act of learning to shelve personal feelings for the priority of the board or, better said, the good of the company. We could write a whole library on the psychological motivations of why we act in certain ways. It takes time and leadership for some to learn to shelve themselves and act as a positive unit. To some degree, this skill can be taught.

HOW TO START A DIRECTOR ON THE RIGHT TRACK

An easier part of a director's job should start before the first meeting. Prior to that meeting, I have any new director scheduled for one long day of briefing. During that day, each department head goes over the what, why, and how of all that takes place in his department. Do not forget the executive and chief operating officer's (CEO's) area. Overall budgets, forecasts, long-range planning, and similar areas are of special interest to a new director.

This gives the new director a broad working knowledge of the company. If this is not done, it may take six months to a year for that director to become his best for you. It is great if you want to sell your ideas and have him vote with you in the boardroom because he does not know any differently. If that is the case, you are playing games again. If you want the best of his creative ability, he has to have more input than a few words of discussion on the motion.

I suggest you have your attorney prepare a two-paragraph layman's explanation of a board member's legal obligations. Announce that once each quarter this will be read at the beginning of a monthly board meeting. In addition, contact your insurance man and have him obtain officers' and directors' liability insurance. If you are new or thin on capital, you had better start this as soon as possible. It may take a while. At the same time, be sure your bylaws have the broadest indemnification clause your state laws will allow. Sharp directors will be concerned with both these items.

Be honest with a prospective member about the time required, exactly what day each month and for how long you meet. Some companies require only two or three hours a month; others, especially where several committees are formed with the board, may require two or three days a month. If the latter is the case, you had better question if that member is becoming involved in management. Be careful, as it is very easy to allow a board member to slip into management responsibilities. An assist toward controlling this may be for the president to hold an executive management meeting a few days before your regular board meeting. Handle all management decisions, then list the board items. Take off that list anything the board does not actually need to know or decide on. Type very brief reports with suggested motions on any of these items for the board. These, along with the regular monthly reports, can then be sent to all directors a few days before the meeting. If they desire to gather further information on any item, they have time. In any case, they can come to the meeting informed and possibly ready to vote with very little time spent on additional discussion. The meeting will go quickly and smoothly.

Another area of education for a director is the dos and don'ts of checking things with staff people. I am sure no member would consider this interference, but it is for sure. Set up a clear line of communication for your directors. There is only one way, through the chairman or, in his absence, possibly through the president; but be sure he knows to keep the chairman completely informed. This must be watched for some directors. The staff generally is not going to come to the president or chairman and complain about a board member. There is an occasional board member who delights in supplying his or her ego by nitpicking and/or in some cases following concerns of real value. In either case keep this person off the staff's back. Take the case of a director, Mr. Nit Picker. He checks the coffee each time he comes in the office. He is pleased with "his" organization if the coffee is always the proper temperature. The problem is, he must have the department head serve as his guide to the kitchen area, and en route they must discuss other superfluous items. Then if the coffee has not been heated to the proper temperature, he, as a director, wants a full report in his hands on all details by 9 A.M. tomorrow. "After all, the entire morale of this company depends on happy employees, and that means good coffee."

As ridiculous as this case may seem, I have seen it happen. Some directors gradually get so entrenched that they wind up with a temporary office that later becomes a permanent facility with secretary.

I would hope that all of your board members are smart. If they have smarts, the other ultimate desire would be for each one to have an abundance of courage. It takes guts to speak out when certain emotional situations confront us. If your member feels secure enough about his self-worth, he will have courage enough to give you the best of his thinking at all times. If you have chosen wisely, your company is likely in good hands.

11

Long-Range Planning—
Forty-Eight Hours

How to Make the Real Money

*Everybody's responsibility is no-
body's responsibility.*

Having lost sight of our objectives, we must double our efforts.

While most presidents would hate to admit publicly that the organization has lost view of its goals, you would be shocked to know how often this is true. Not long ago, I was doing a consulting job for a firm that does $25 million a year in sales in company-owned stores. They had called me in to make recommendations with regard to setting up a franchising operation. On my second day there, I separately asked three different mid-management people about their department and overall company objectives. They stumbled all over possible answers. They were pulling at straws. They did not have a clear picture.

Long-range (LR) and short-range (SR) planning usually can have dramatic effects on changing or improving a direction. I thoroughly agree with Rene Dubois, who said, "Trend is not destiny." We can direct our companies to desired destinies by analyzing where we are now, where we have been, why, and where we want to go. By considering all known effects and then planning, we can reach that destiny one step at a time.

One often views the big picture and fails to plan the next small step in that big direction. A mountain cannot be climbed by one giant step. It takes a lot of little steps to get to the top.

HOW TO PLAN YOUR WORK AND WORK YOUR PLAN

Plan your work and work your plan. That is probably one of the most often-mentioned prescriptions for effective management. Its value seems so obvious. No executive can find fault with it. Then why do so many companies find it difficult to get around to planning? Possibly because such a large number of CEOs have not tasted the success that comes from having planned or because they usually feel they do have plans. True, they may have ideas of general directions, but in fact, their objectives are not well defined. By not having objectives detailed on paper, their people progress much more slowly at their tasks. Efforts are greatly dissipated.

If you would like to see if this is true with your company, Mr. C.E.O., ask the people in two or three departments to write down the purposes and goals of the company, with the general steps in reaching same. They should do this separately and without communicating with each other. You will be shocked at the results. But don't get upset at your people—you are the one at fault if they do not know. Accept the challenge and do something to bring about positive change.

An organization that does not plan for its future is not likely to have one. First, let me clear up a common error in thinking. Planning is not forecasting. We do not actually plan the future, but instead plan for (or prepare for) the future. In long-range planning, we should not attempt to deal with future decisions. We are attempting to make decisions today, with today's knowledge, which will affect our company's future positively and profitably. In other words, we are making decisions now in an effort to make the future go in the direction we desire.

These step-by-step decisions cannot be sequenced today unless we have a formula to get us through. We must be able to arrive at a point with certain facts and base conclusions in order to make intelligent decisions. In other words, we must have a management schedule for long-range planning.

We cannot afford to allow tomorrow to take care of itself. The smaller company will say, "That is important to the big company, but not so much to me." Wrong! No matter what the company's size, effective planning helps greatly to guarantee survival. Maybe *survival* is too strong a word. Perhaps I should say if you want to get bigger the easiest way possible, in the shortest period of time, and make the most profit while doing it, get going on a long-range management plan.

It is impossible to explain in this chapter what starts off by taking a week of concentrated effort and then follows up with three to six months of directional effort to complete. In general, I will lay out the planning process. You cannot actually complete a plan from this outline, but you can perhaps develop a feeling for what it entails.

HOW TO PICK YOUR PLANNING TEAM

First, we must comprise the planning team. Twelve or fewer people in the world are qualified to write the plan for your company's future. This applies to almost any size company. The CEO, his top executives, and some of your directors are the only people qualified. They:

1. Supply the facts.
2. Do the actual planning layout.
3. Create the plan itself.
4. Authorize the plan actions.

As a result of the team planning process, management winds up with:

1. A written guide for actual steps to be taken in day-to-day development toward realistic objectives.
2. Detailed action plans, specifically assigned, with completion dates, costs, and analysis of benefits.
3. A planned set of decisions on strategically important matters that are vital to the company's future.
4. A set of benchmarks to monitor future sales, profits, expenses, and growth, as well as the dozens of uncontrollables that exist both inside and outside the company.
5. Realistic and specific estimates of the capital, manpower, and facilities to handle each action plan, whether now or in the future.
6. Solid conclusions in regard to what may happen to the marketplace, raw materials, monetary gyrations, inflation, equity markets, and numerous other important areas.
7. Contingency plans to help you react quickly to unexpected developments in the industry, in the marketplace, in the economy, or in society at large.
8. A system of control which assures a continuing and vital planning effort.

9. New planning knowledge and techniques for your top people, who can then extend these skills within the company. They can revise the plan if necessary to cope with an unpredictable future.
10. A sense of unity among your top team. They now have common vocabulary, shared values, and feelings of true teamwork.

Probably for the first time everyone in the company will be thinking in the same direction. The fact that you have been in a board meeting and heard different philosophies of managment come forward should show you how important a plan is. There should be only one unified philosophy.

BENEFITS OF THE PLAN

Since all agree and are aiming in the same direction, other benefits become highly visible.

1. Goals are reached faster.
2. Goals are reached with better results.
3. Cooperation among personnel whose ideas are all the same brings greater personal satisfaction and, thus, greater individual productivity.
4. There is less personnel turnover.
5. Costly mistakes are often avoided.
6. Flexibility for future change is achieved with more solid assurance of correctness.

THE CRITICAL STEPS IN THE PLANNING PROCESS

Now let's lay out the steps in the planning process. The CEO can make or break any plan. His decision to commit himself and his staff to the process is absolutely critical. The beginning steps are:

I. Select six to twelve of your top people to participate as the planning team.
II. The goals and steps of the process are outlined exactly by your outstanding leader so the team understands what is expected.

III. Preliminary fact-gathering assignments are made to accumulate data needed for the planning sessions.

IV. Develop a planning base:
   A. Internal analysis of:
      1. Mission and purpose of the company: A statement as to what business you are in and want to be in during the range of the plan period.
      2. Policies and beliefs: General statements or understandings which guide and channel the thinking and decisions of the planners. Naturally, the ultimate policies are decided by the board of directors and the CEO. (E.g., We will not sell to the government. We will maintain a debt-to-equity ratio not to exceed ½ to 1. Any acquisition must yield 15 percent before tax (B/T) return on investment (ROI), etc.)
      3. Historical performance: Management's approach, style, and effectiveness. All of this is a matter of record when applying the facts and figures against policies from 2 above.
      4. Current game plan: Outline of the present plans as they "formally" exist.
      5. Organization structure: The nature of the company, its manpower resources, and its fundamental characteristics.
      6. Management style and philosophy:
         a) Is it now management by objectives?
         b) How do the staff people understand management's philosophy of running things?
      7. Strengths, weaknesses, problems, needs, opportunities:
         a) Detailed outlines of all these begin to bring key facts uniformly to light.
         b) External analysis of competitive factors: What is the industry struucture in general? In connection with your top five competitors, where do you stand with regard to:
            (1) Price
            (2) Locations
            (3) Service
            (4) Name Recognition
            (5) Appearance
            (6) Marketing
            (7) Sign Graphics
            (8) Size of Your Business
            (9) Sales

   c) Weighted evaluation of all of *b)* above to form a con-
    clusion of your strengths and weaknesses.
   d) After concluding *c)* above, what areas can be exploited?
    (1) Environmental factors:
     (a) Political
     (b) Social
     (c) Economical
     (d) Technological
    (2) In connection with *(a)* through *(d)* above, decide:
     (a) Major trends and conditions.
     (b) Future assumptions.
     (c) The impact on your business.
     (d) What should be your response.

V. Identity:
 A. Threats and opportunities:
  1. Assess the impact of trends and developments on the company.
  2. What action or response should the company make to these?
  3. Are there critical business factors that need immediate actions?

VI. Translate planning base into a preliminary plan
 A. First phase:
  1. Review, confirm, modify, and draft the mission and strategic guidelines for future corporate development.
   a) Mission
   b) Policies
   c) Beliefs
   d) Values
   e) Principles
   f) Objectives
    (1) General (continuing)
    (2) Specific (near term)
  2. Develop base-line forecast.
  3. Determine the gaps if principle objectives are to be reached.
 B. Second phase:
  1. Develop programs to achieve the objectives (close the gaps).
  2. Classify the various action plans to support the gap-closing programs.
  3. Establish priorities for projects.

       4.   Identify additional data to be obtained.

       5.   Make work assignments with respect to objectives, programs, and action plans.

       6.   Assign responsibility and due dates for completion of above.

  C.   Third phase: Establish check points to review action plans to see that everyone is on track and on schedule in preparing their plans.

VII.   Review, evaluation, finalization:

  A.   Review and summarize assignments.

       1.   Confirm objectives, guidelines, and strategies as now seen by all planners.

       2.   Review and validate action plans, resource requirements, resource capabilities, benefits.

  B.   Rank action plans according to priority in relation to goals.

  C.   Determine need for contingency programs and design accordingly.

  D.   Control Procedures:

       1.   Schedules

       2.   Planning at lower levels

       3.   Performance evaluation

       4.   Reviews and updates

  E.   Draft the Final Written Plans.

After all this, you need to set up a schedule to review the company's performance. You will reevaluate goals and benchmarks. There will be new threats identified in the future as well as new opportunities and critical issues. Since this is definite, you will be drawing up new action plans and new assessments for your company's future as time goes by.

WHO SHOULD GUIDE YOU IN A PLANNING PROCESS?

There are important decisions that must precede the organization of any planning session. First, do not attempt to hold a planning session without an outside moderator/leader, never a member of your own company. It must be someone who is experienced in planning and who is in no way personally involved with your company, your people, or your profitability. Soul-searching yet objective analysis of the present situation and position is a must. With an outside leader only clear, unemotional objectivity verging on self-criticism will be allowed rather than excuses.

The second requirement is for the planning sessions to be conducted in a distraction-free environment totally away from office and home. It must be fifty miles or more away. The first session should take five consecutive days, from 9 A.M. to 9 P.M. Next comes two to five months of information gathering. Last, there will be a session of three to five days to evaluate and finalize the plan.

My company did this. We managed to do well in years prior to starting long-range planning. We felt good about our growth and profits. But I can assure you that going through the planning sessions is probably the finest thing we ever did to maximize our growth, progress, and profits.

KEY FORMS TO GET THE JOB DONE

ACTION PLAN

DATE _____

REVISION _____

REVISION _____

AUTHOR _____

PLAN TITLE: _____

DUE DATE _____

OBJECTIVE:

	RESPONSIBILITY OF	DATE TO BE COMPLETED	COMPLETED DATE

ACTION PLAN *(continued)*

	1985	1986	1987	1988	1989
IMPACT ON INCOME					
COST-OPERATING SG & A					
CAPITAL NEEDED					
MANPOWER NEEDED					
PRESENT BUDGET					
ASSUMPTIONS:					

SUMMARY OF
ACTION PLAN ASSIGNMENTS

PLAN	RESPONSIBILITY OF	DATE TO BE COMPLETED

THE KEY TO GROWTH

The following graph applies to almost anything large, small, individual or group, company or government. The Main Interest for business may be profits; for an individual it may be leisure time or personal income. The important word is "main" interest. Try it on yourself or your company.

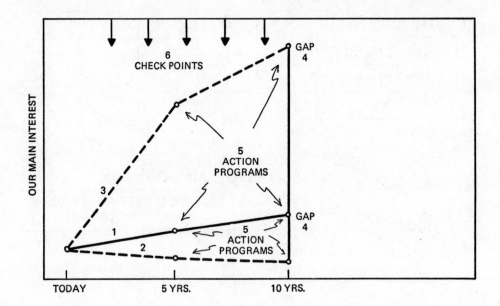

12

Sink or Swim, Black or White, Believe It or Not

How to Put the Two Necessary Contracts Together

*If you think education is expensive
...try ignorance.*

Remember that saying, "Those who have failed to learn lessons from the past, may be forced to relive them." Running a franchising company is like walking through fresh snow: Every step shows. Thus, whatever you do should be undertaken as if the whole world were watching...it is.

YOUR FRANCHISE CONTRACT

Let us first take a look at one of the starting tools of your trade, your franchise contract or license, as it often is called. You really have two contracts which you must constantly deal with. One is the *legal contract*, with which everyone is familiar. The other contract is the *implied contract of human relations*. Without harmony between the two, the greatest rewards cannot be reaped by you, your franchisees, and probably their customers as well.

The legal contract could be 75–100 pages long. It could cover every possible situation. But if the other contract (of human relations) and the ability to develop that contract are not present, then quite often it is not worth the cost of enforcing the legal contract for the rewards that can be reaped.

WHICH CONTRACT IS MOST IMPORTANT

I suggest that you train yourself to reach first for the human relations approach and not for the legal contract. Examine ways to bring about reasonable dialogue.

In doing consulting work and from experiences with my company, I can attest to the benefits of going to see a franchisee personally if there should be points of difference. Sit face to face with him. It can be doubly rewarding to stay out of legal fights and keep an existing franchisee.

The ancient Greeks had what they called the Code of Citizenship: "The City of Athens should be a better place when a citizen leaves the city than when he arrived." He was taught public responsibility, to become a public citizen. It was the concept of the public citizen, not the private citizen. Each citizen was there to improve his city and thereby improve his own personal lot in life.

As a franchisor, keep close guard on this code of the wise Greeks. At every turn you must remember to consider the lot of the franchisee and his customers as well as your own company. I realize you are a profit-making organization, but like the Athenian philosophy, by improving the lot of the franchisee you will usually improve your own.

Once I was going over a company's franchise agreement. It read easily but was loaded with every possible thought to cover and double-cover the franchisor. I had a feeling this contract was probably causing the sales department problems. Upon checking, I was correct. Potential franchisees were being scared away by the agreement. I sat down with the company executives and their attorney and went over the contract paragraph by paragraph. They found there were many paragraphs that were actually of no real importance to the company.

HOW TO GO ABOUT CHANGING CONTRACTS

When I asked them to imagine themselves as potential franchisees reading the contract, they understood and found several more areas to take out or change. We often do not work on the human relations portion of our contracts. A certain amount of protection and legal wording is asbolutely necessary—just be sure it represents the real world of practicalities.

Know also that the contract of two years ago probably needs deletion, change, and addition. This does not necessarily mean the old contract was wrong; it merely means change may be advisable. Learning to recognize, accept, and make change is one of senior management's top jobs. There are several ways you can handle change.

One way to handle change is as an offensive attacker. Set certain dates each year to formally define and lay out plans for attacking changes. This approach is true of the company that stays ahead of the competition, that innovates, that is the industry leader—the company others copy.

The other way would be as a defensive changer. This is typified by the company president who changes because his competition has changed and he wants to try to protect what he has. This company could certainly not be considered a leader of change. It probably is a copier.

Change is viewed by some as a threat. Again, design the presentation of change with human relations factors in mind. Allow the words to give honesty and clarity; forthrightly state exactly what you mean. Usually your changes will then be less threatening to others concerned.

HOW IMPORTANT THE HUMAN RELATIONS CONTRACT CAN BE

Finally, let me tell you a true story about how important the contract of human relations can be to a franchisor. In 1973 there were two franchising companies. We will call one Acme Company and the other Best Company. Both companies had approximately eighty-five outlets, they operated in the same geographic area of the United States, their names were very similar, and they were both in the same type of business, with practically everything else alike. The gas crunch hit in the fall of 1973, and in 1974 the economy went on its back. Both companies had franchisees who were starting to hurt financially. The franchisees began to slack off on paying their royalties.

The Acme Company talked to those franchisees who fell behind a couple of times and then pulled out of the legal franchise contract. It said when and how much the franchisees were supposed to pay. Acme Company said they wanted their money. Next, the attorneys started collection proceedings. Suits were filed. The franchisees filed counter-suits; a three-ring circus began in the courtroom. The franchisees were mad by now. They withheld their franchise fees altogether. The court cases strung out and as a result, Acme Company wound up in bankruptcy. The company fell apart, and thus the franchisees lost as well. There they were without a unified system. Many of the franchisees also wound up in bankruptcy.

Now let us look at Best Company. They were involved in the same situation, but instead of calling in attorneys for the legal contract collections, they called in the franchisees. They sat down together. There were harsh words at times, but the company kept its cool. They even suggested that the franchisees recommend someone to come on Best Company's board of directors. This way the franchisees could have direct input and, perhaps more important, direct feedback. It became an educational process for both sides. As a result, pay-out terms for back royalties were worked out, fears were stilled by the inside knowledge of true facts, and today Best Company is doing very well. The human relations contract saved the company that recognized and respected it.

I do not have socialistic tendencies. In fact, I have strong leanings in the opposite direction. Likewise, I do not advocate giving away the store. Good common sense and wise business judgments are their own rewards. Rewards in profits, in all areas of growth, in working relationships and personal satisfactions are all expected. "I find the more I take out of my basket and put in someone else's, the more I have in my basket."

13

Do You Really Believe the Customer Is King?

We are not as good as we hope to be, but we are better than we used to be. (That means we aren't as bad as we were.)

There were three customers lined up for a young clerk to wait on them. The third person was a man of about forty who had observed the hurried and almost rude behavior of the clerk. When the clerk started to give him the same treatment, he stopped her sharply and said, "I think you have things mixed up a little, young lady. You see, you are the overhead here, and I am the profit."

It we could get this one point across to all of our people, we would have success in the bag. I guess it comes down to "How much do you believe it?" It is not enough to teach the words to your people. While that is a necessity, it is more important to exemplify it in your every attitude. What is your attitude when you design a new policy for franchisees? For your company employees? For yourself? Are there different measures, different tolerances you allow? Do you ever try to put something over just because you think you have an advantage or can get by with it? Is your system of values firmly planted with honest, logical humanistic business attitudes?

What does all this have to do with the customer? Plenty! The ideal you emulate is transposed through your people to the franchisees and on down to the customer/user. Your sole existence in this relationship is balanced upon having the right relationship with the customer, the end user of your product or service. Often we become so immersed in our franchisor relationship that we neglect the ultimate consumers—perhaps not intentionally, or even to a great extent, but any extent is costly.

We are in a relationship of dependency. It is a continued dependency. Therefore, we must stay aware of that relationship at all times. The customers' likes of two years ago may be different today. The change may come about as a result of media or competition, social customs, economics, or a number of other reasons. Whatever it is, you should be aware of it when or before the trend line starts to bend.

WHY DEMOGRAPHICS ARE IMPORTANT

No matter what area of business you are in, the ultimate user should be your king. You should constantly be aware of what and where your market is. The demographics of your ultimate user are the crystal ball that can save you many thousands of dollars, and will earn you the same.

Demographics are a must when it comes to advertising. In a free enterprise system of economics, no one holds a gun to anyone's head and says they must buy from you. Your advertising must do the job. If you lack accurate market and customer statistics you may lose a bundle. I'm not saying you cannot do well on gut feelings; I'm saying you will make less than you could have.

On the other hand, you could have a great set of statistics, plan a beautiful marketing program, and fail. I know a company that did just that. This company did a beautiful job of demographics. They had well-placed locations. The marketing program was superb. They began with a big bang in about twenty locations all on the same day in a well-defined region.

The advertising pulled the customers into the fast food outlets. During the first two months it was not unusual to see people five to ten deep lined up at each cash register. That was part of the problem! The employees were not thoroughly trained and service was less than customers would like. In addition, the product was only fair to good in comparison with competition. The customer became king, voted "no", and in twelve months all twenty fast food outlets were out of business. A beautiful beginning if you want to count customers for only two months; but a bad, bad finish.

Be sure you believe and convey the message that the customer is king. "It used to be I couldn't spell 'customer'...now I are one." They come from all around.

14

How Will a Potential Franchisee Evaluate Your Franchise?

What You Should Put into Your Franchise System

If you were someone else, would you like to be a friend of yours?

I doubt seriously that you have ever had a close friend you have not shared very personal feelings with. That is one of the ways one becomes a close friend. When it comes to sharing, the same is true of a potential franchisee. He undoubtedly knows far less about your business than you do. By sharing information, or interest in his needs, you stand the best chance of making a sale. Note I said an interest in *his* needs. There again, we must know our franchisee/customer demographics in order to be able to design your sales literature best.

Generally, a potential franchisee is looking for: (A) a convenient and economic means for filling a drive or desire for independence or greater financial rewards, and (B) a minimum of risk and involvement and maximum opportunities for success through the utilization of a proven product or service and marketing method. This is a general statement and may have to be more refined for your specific business, but it is usually fairly accurate.

To continue with generalities, we realize the potential franchisee must give up some freedom in his business decisions that a nonfranchise owner would have. In some ways, a franchisee owner is not totally his own boss. He must abide by the requirements of the franchisor. In return, the potential franchisee would share in the good will and other benefits which have been built by the franchisor and the other franchisees.

THIRTY-FOUR THINGS POTENTIAL FRANCHISEES LOOK FOR

Some of the items potential franchisees will be looking for and you might want to cover are:

1. Area selection assistance
2. Unit location analysis
3. Unit development aid
4. Lease or purchase assistance
5. Unit design
6. Equipment layout and design
7. Employee and management training
8. Continued training
9. Controls on standardized operations
10. Mass centralized purchasing savings
11. Business financial assistance
12. Territory, if any
13. Termination
14. Royalty fees
15. Initial franchise fee
16. Franchise sale requirements
17. Opinions of existing franchisees
18. Reputation for fair dealing with franchisees and user/customer
19. Cost and earning figures

20. Marketing program
21. Compliance with state registrations
22. Compliance with FTC registration
23. Capital requirements
24. Competition
25. Franchisors' position in the market
26. Franchisors' position to acquire more of the market
27. Personal time requirements
28. Success ratios of other franchisors
29. Basic franchise/franchisor relations policies
30. Trademarks and trade name protection
31. In what litigation have the principals and/or the franchisor been involved
32. Rehabilitation policies
33. Renewal of franchise
34. Business relations and financial references

Everyone is aware that there are risks in any venture. There are some franchises that have greater risks than others. For the potential franchisee, the risk may be greater than investing in the stock market because often one is not only investing one's money, but one's time and perhaps life's work. Therefore, one must rely on the business skills of the franchisor... so tell them.

Tell them also about how you are investing in them. Tell them about how the benefits come to you, but only over an extended period of time. Explain the importance for both of you in having the right match.

Finally, recommend that they consult with their attorney and/or CPA. Sometimes this message is tough to convey, but this is a special caution spot. I have seen many things blown apart by well-meaning professionals. The policy I personally follow with my consultants is: "Do not tell me whether or not to go into the deal. That is a business decision that I will make. Only tell me from a legal or accounting standpoint whether it is okay or needs to be changed." While some attorneys or CPAs may become upset with this, if they have their heads screwed on straight, they will understand and agree with you. Convey this point to your potential franchisee, especially if he is somewhat new in the business world. If you do not, his advisor may kill the deal because of lack of knowledge.

By sharing as much as is practical with the potential franchisee, you have a better chance of him becoming a franchisee and a friend...just be sure what you share is 125 percent correct.

15

Can Consultants Help and
Are They Worth It?

The Fastest, Best, Least Expensive Way to Be Successful

Anything is possible if you do not know what you are talking about.

Even though I do consulting work, I have trouble when I think about the profession. How can anyone be a consultant in the highly specialized field of franchising if they have never actually been in the franchising field for themselves? I know one can learn basic principles from books or learn over a period of time by doing consulting. Thus you are "going to school and learning on the dollars of others." But is that fair to the franchisor client? I do not think so. It is enough for the franchisor to pay a consultant, but to have to pay for the good and bad judgments he makes while he is going to school on you is not fair. I am sure this is not what the consultant disclosed to the franchisor.

Personally, I never consult in any area where I have not had experience in real life. If someone has invested his or her own money and time over the years to learn which media works for which type of business and what day of the week produces the most leads, or how to expand by subfranchising, or how to meet the payroll each week, then he or she has some credentials beyond book theory, and has paid for any errors with his or her own dollars. He or she has thus learned the correct way and, having paid for same, has valuable knowledge to sell as a consultant.

Now this does not mean I have not learned much from the companies to which I have been exposed as a consultant. I certainly have. The accumulation of this knowledge is a large part of this book. After all, no one lives long enough, or has money enough, to make all the mistakes available to him or her.

I certainly do not mean for this chapter to become a commercial for or against consultants. The watch words are, "be careful." One definition of consultant might be, "A consultant is a person brought in to find out what has gone wrong by the people who made it go wrong, in the comfortable expectation that he will not bite the hand that feeds him by placing the blame where it belongs."

I know this is what some management people have in mind when they call me in. I like to turn this around quickly by refusing to dwell solely on what went wrong. It is important, but I want to know how we can make something positive out of where they are now.

I have found many companies with problems have developed functional blindness to their own efforts. They are suffering, not because they cannot solve their problems, but because they cannot see their problems. When they are made to see their difficulties, they spend too much time wallowing in them, because they lack the creativity and experience to choose the next solid step without fear of another problem developing. This is one area where the consultant becomes very valuable. He has knowledge of the next solid step.

The very fact that you are in or considering franchising is a testimonial to consulting. Franchising is one of the purest examples of the value of having a consultant as a guide. The "consultant" Franchisor is responsible for the high success ratio for those who choose to operate under a franchise versus becoming an independent in business.

The franchisor has first done it himself. He knows the dos and don'ts because of trial and error. He has spent time and money to find the correct answers. He has earned his stripes and thus become a consultant to guide new franchisees. There we have some of the main reasons for the high success ratio for franchising.

In addition, we have the testimony for your greater success if you choose a consultant wisely. Be sure your consultant, like the franchisor, has done it for himself first. Dwell on that thought when considering a consultant: If you were a potential franchisee, would you be reluctant to trust your savings to a franchisor who had no track record of having operated successfully? The same goes when considering a potential consultant.

One of the basic benefits a consultant can render involves the forest and the trees. A consultant can view the organization more objectively than can insiders. As an outsider, he can see things you cannot. He can touch politically sensitive areas where insiders dare not tread.

The consultant's experience of contacts with many other companies is like having the benefits of much of the good without the bad. Those experiences of successes are what you want. Why go to the expense and time to recreate the wheel?

There are other important factors to consider. Exactly who in the consultant's organization will do your work? Is the consultant himself involved, or is the work detailed out to others on staff? Has it been pinned down in writing exactly what is expected? How are the costs figured and what is the estimate on the particular job? How much time will it take to do each phase? In what form and when will the conclusions come? How much detail is desired? What staff and executive help will be expected of your company? How much disruption will the consultant cause in your organization?

After this simple and direct approach to consulting, I will go into the more academic side for those who prefer the one-two-three system as a guide.

In any relationship with a consultant, it is important that the consultant continue to function as an independent outsider rather than a part of management. The consultant's role is to advise, recommend, and provide specialized knowledge. A professional consultant avoids making decisions. He urges and persuades clients toward a sound course of action.

It is up to management to weigh the recommendations, modify them if necessary to fit particular circumstances, make the final decisions, and assume responsibility for them. Any implication or erroneous impression that management has abdicated its function and responsibilities, or that decisions are being made by others not finally responsible to the stockholders, should be avoided.

WHAT A GOOD CONSULTANT DOES

A good consultant will suggest that the client's staff be trained properly to carry on certain activities. This eliminates the needless expense of the consultant providing services the client can and should perform without outside help. A reliable consultant does not indulge in make-work activities for his own benefit.

After pointing out the principal value of consultants, it is only proper to mention difficulties that some companies have had with consulting services. Clients may find themselves dissatisfied with consultants for a variety of reasons. They may complain that consultants lack experience, are too young, are not qualified, or charge too much. They may feel that consultants have used high-pressure selling tactics; in some cases, they may find that the consultant hired away one of their best employees. Perhaps a consultant may have wanted a client just so he could add that name to his list of references.

Some clients may be let down because the consultant only picked the brains of their people and put these opinions in a fancy report. "He didn't tell us anything we didn't already know. He didn't contribute any new approach."

The things some consultants suggest may be too theoretical. "We were at a loss when we tried to figure out how to implement his recommendations. There was no way to make them pay off in practical results. He came in and installed prepackaged solutions to problems. He was not aware, and didn't make himself aware, of particular needs."

A few consultants have been incompetent. "We felt we were teaching a relatively young, inexperienced man who was operating by the book, and we resented the fee."

These problem areas may be avoided by taking proper care in selecting, working with, and measuring the work of consultants. Not all comments are negative. Many firms which use consultants testify that costly mistakes and risks of failure have been reduced through the counseling of qualified people.

What procedures should be followed in order to select a properly qualified consultant? In every profession, some are more scrupulous in their standards of conduct and practice than others. There are as yet no professional standards of qualification in franchise consulting which enable clients to differentiate well-qualified consultants from incompetent or unethical practitioners. Here are some ideas you might try.

CHECKLIST FOR CHOOSING A CONSULTANT

1. Check the general reputation of the consultant as a normal part of your preliminary search for consulting help. Although a reputation is a useful guide, it must continue to be earned. A good recommendation from someone you know or from an organization you respect is a very good way to start.

2. The consultant should be financially sound. The consultant's bank, Dun & Bradstreet, Standard and Poors, the Better Business Bureau, and credit associations should be checked if you do not have a good recommendation from someone you know.

3. Prepare an outline of the nature, scope, and purposes of the assignment. Such a statement will assist in selecting the most suitable consultant. It will also help the consultant to present his or her qualifications in relation to the job. Some consultants dig into other areas often unrelated to their original assignment. This can be avoided by an understanding of the scope of the work. Like managing, analytical consulting is a professional field with its own skills, practices, and techniques. Many good teachers of business administration do not make good business operators. The question to ask is, "How good is the consultant at franchise consulting?"

4. You want a professional and experienced franchise consultant to pin down and analyze the problems and suggest what can be done. If you are not pleased with the first interview, you should consider the general qualifications of more than one consultant who appears to be capable.

5. Thought should be given to the advantages and disadvantages inherent in the size of the consulting firm. Here are some questions to consider:

- Does the premise that the company's problems will receive more attention from the principals of a small firm outweigh the facilities a large firm possesses?
- Is the problem such that employing a "name" will carry greater weight with bankers, the company's board, or prospective customers?
- Could the problem be solved by a qualified individual consultant who designates specialists to handle specifics such as legal, accounting, data processing, and so on, and merely supervises the results?
- When selecting a consultant, keep in mind that the heart of the consulting process lies in the analysis and solution of problems by an independent and objective professional. It is not necessarily valid that consultants who have specific knowledge and experience in your kind of business, profession, or industry are better for your job. In fact, the opposite may be true. Remember that a consultant's competence in a technical area does not guarantee ability in organizational planning. Recognize that a consultant may have developed the ability to analyze and solve problems without necessarily being

conversant with the details of your business. You need not emphasize the consultant's previous experience with the exact problem in the exact kind of business or industry as much as his record of success in solving difficult franchisor problems.

WHAT DO CONSULTANTS CHARGE?

What are the financial arrangements for consultants? In calculating fees, a consultant to franchisors should include the principal costs involved in the assignment, such as travel, subsistence, materials, supplies, services, special research, and the like. Beware of consultants who offer free services or guarantee results or savings, or propose a fee contingent on the findings or results of services. Such inducements are not sound professional practice. Reputable consultants make their professional experience available to clients and serve them to the best of their ability. Those who promise more are unfaithful to the best interests of clients.

Knowledgeable clients realize they cannot get services for nothing. It is difficult for the consultant to be objective when he receives a request for a free survey. Once the consultant has made an investment in free survey time, he will probably feel obligated to recommend the further use of his services, whether needed or not, to recover his investment.

It is not possible to identify standard fee schedules governing the charges of consultants because of variables in the extent of the consultant's education and experience, the variety of work in which he or she has successfully engaged, and the quality and character of his or her specialization. Consultants with established reputations, or those who are more competent in certain areas, may demand higher fees because of the special services they can render.

Good franchise consulting is not inexpensive. Highly skilled people are required, whose fees must be measured against the competition of the high specialized salaries in industry. Some of the fee arrangements that are used are these:

1. The *per diem* or *hourly fee* is probably the most common method of fee setting for a specific, short, detailed job.
2. The *standard quotation* involves a minimum and maximum fee, with the understanding that the work will be accomplished unless unforeseen conditions arise.
3. The *lump sum* or *fixed amount contract* is generally for a sum which includes both per diem fees and out-of-pocket expenses.

4. The *retainer* is a method by which the client reserves a certain amount of the consultant's time, usually for a year, when the work contemplated cannot be detailed in advance.

5. The *contingent fee* involves work by the consultant on the basis of compensation to be determined later, depending on the benefits that accrue from the service. It is not usually a desirable method of setting fees, and professional consultants rarely use it.

A fee may sound high or low—it depends on where you stand. Just remember, "If you think education is expensive, try failure."

16

Getting Help with Laws and Regulations

Important Names and Addresses in Franchise Law

If everyone was put on earth for a special purpose, I wonder why it is that no one knows what they are doing?

Someone once said if laws could speak for themselves, they would complain about lawyers. This seems true, especially from a layman's view as he first comes in contact with the regulations placed upon our business. "To be or not be be" is no longer the question. The question today is "how?"

We have become immersed in a sea of papers that is almost incomprehensible. The Ten Commandments, the rules of life for all mankind, consist of less than one hundred words. The Lord's Prayer has only seventy-two words. The Declaration of Independence is amazingly short. Yet, years later, the U.S. Government's *Mergers and Acquisitions Regulations of the Securities Exchange Commission* consists of 138,252 words. Now another type of consultant must be brought on the scene: an attorney.

HOW TO PICK THE ATTORNEYS

Here is where I must make a disclaimer (to use legal language). The following is my personal opinion; I believe it to be shared by most franchising chief executive officers who have been in the business four years or more: Get a specialist in franchise law.

This does not threaten your local corporate counsel. You will need him to do loads of other things as well as work with the specialist. Do not allow your local counsel to do all your franchise contract work or registrations unless he has time in the business of franchising and has been exposed to seminars such as the legal symposium conducted each May by the International Franchise Association (IFA) in Washington, D.C. Any other action will probably cost plenty at some future date.

In your wildest dreams you probably cannot imagine the complications you can get into in franchise law. The seemingly simplest thing can become a millstone that will haunt you for years to come. This is where an experienced business consultant can guide you, suggesting ways of accomplishing solutions without costing you an arm and leg in legal fees.

Franchising is an investment business and therefore is more open to greedy or unscrupulous opportunists. Thus, the government has stepped in with controls and regulations. Franchising has matured over recent years to the point where its regulations resemble those placed upon the securities field. Both franchising and securities aim for disclosure to protect the investor. Many may agree that the recent Federal Trade Commission (FTC) ruling on disclosure has given additional credibility to our industry.

In 1970 California became the first state to require disclosure and registration. Also in 1970 Delaware passed the first termination and nonrenewal legislation at the state level. In 1971 the FTC Rule was introduced. In 1974 the IFA endorsed the Uniform Franchise Offering Circular (UFOC).

THE FTC FRANCHISING RULE

Finally, after nearly seven years of debate, consideration, and compromise, the FTC franchising rule became law. It preempted many aspects and also covered those states that had not yet adopted statutes. Because of the interrelationship with federal and state laws and rules, it usually requires the services of an attorney to put together the compliance documents.

Some of the areas of disclosure involve information concerning:

1. Directors and executive officers
2. Litigation and bankrupt histories

3. The franchise offered
4. Initial fees
5. Future royalties/fees
6. Purchasing requirements
7. Required personal participation
8. Past cancellation statistics
9. Past renewal statistics
10. Past termination statistics
11. Type of training offered
12. Assistance in site selection
13. Financial statistics
14. Description of the franchise
15. Business experience of the franchisor
16. Sales restrictions

Since violation of the FTC Rule may result in penalties of up to $10,000 per violation per day, it behooves everyone to be in compliance and have their salespeople properly instructed in the dos and don'ts. One of the best recommendations I can give you here is to join the IFA. The assistance you get in the legal area alone will save you many times the annual fee. The seminars, workshops, and general business assistance are bonuses you must have to be as successful as possible.

HOW TO TELL IF YOU ARE INVOLVED IN FRANCHISING

Numerous times I have had the question posed, "Would my business be considered a franchise?" Generally, the following is what the FTC and several state laws consider a franchise. It is any business relationship in which:

1. The franchisor's marketing system or plan significantly assists or controls the franchisee.
2. The franchisor receives a fee from the franchisee.
3. The franchisor grants the right to use his trademark to the franchisee.

To some extent, the FTC Rule and many state franchise laws exempt product business relationships from being considered franchises. One must be careful, however, in that some special industry legislation may make that product business involvement a franchise. Typical product franchises would be soft drink bottlers, service stations, and automobile dealerships.

The other type of franchise is the package or business format franchise. They include personnel agencies, motels and hotels, fast food operations, convenient food stores, and many others we have grown to know over the last two or three decades.

Franchise law has grown since 1970 by leaps and bounds. As an example, the IFA published *Franchise Laws, Regulations and Rulings* in two volumes totaling about 600 pages in 1976. The 1980 printing consisted of four volumes which totaled over 2,000 pages. In addition, supplements come out almost monthly.

IDENTIFYING STATES WITH FRANCHISE AND BUSINESS OPPORTUNITY LAWS

Following are the agencies that administer state franchise and business opportunity laws:

California

Department of Corporations
600 S. Commonwealth Ave.
Los Angeles CA 90005
(213) 736-2741

1025 P Street, Room 205
Sacramento CA 95814
(916) 445-7205

1350 Front Street, Room 2034
San Diego CA 92101
(714) 237-7341

1390 Market St.
San Francisco, CA 94108
(415) 557-3787

Hawaii (filing, not registration)

Department of Regulatory Agencies and Securities
1010 Richards Street
Honolulu HI 96813
(217) 782-1279

Illinois

Chief Franchise Division
Attorney General's Office
500 S. Second Street
Springfield, IL 62706
(217) 782-1279

Indiana

Deputy Commissioner
Franchise Division
Indiana Securities Division
Secretary of State
Suite 560
N. Capitol St.
Indianapolis IN 46204
(317) 232-6681

Maryland

Assistant Attorney General
Maryland Division of Securities
2nd Floor, The Munsey Bldg.
2 N. Calvert Street, Room 602
Baltimore MD 21202
(301) 576-6360

Michigan (filing, not registration)

Franchise Administration
Antitrust & Franchise Unit
Economic Crime Division
Michigan Attorney General
6520 Mercantile Way
Suite 3
Lansing MI 48913
(517) 373-3800

Minnesota

Minnesota Department of Commerce
500 Metro Square Building
St. Paul MN 55101
(612) 296-2594

New York

Bureau of Investor Protection & Securities
New York State Department of Law
2 World Trade Center, Room 4825A
New York NY 10047
(212) 488-7415

North Dakota

Franchise Examiner
Office of Securities Commission
State Capitol Building
Third Floor
Bismarck ND 58501
(701) 224-2910

Rhode Island

Chief Securities Examiner
Securities Section
Banking Division
100 N. Main Street
Providence RI 02903
(401) 277-2405

South Dakota

Franchise Administration
Division of Securities
State Capitol Building
Pierre SD 57501
(605) 773-4013

Virginia

Examination Coordinator
Franchise Section
Division of Securities and Retail Franchising
11 South 12th Street
Richmond VA 23219
(804) 786-7751 or 786-1318

Washington

Registration Attorney
Department of Licensing
Business and Professions Administration
Securities Division
P. O. Box 648
Olympia WA 98504
(206) 753-6928

Wisconsin

Chief Attorney
Commissioner of Securities
Franchise Investment Division
P. O. Box 1768
Madison WI 53701
(608) 266-3414

The following offices administer business opportunity laws:

California

Office of the Secretary of State
"Seller Assisted Marketing Plan"
1230 J Street
Sacramento CA 95814
(916) 445-0620

Connecticut

Department of Banking
Securities Division
165 Capitol Avenue
Hartford CT 06106
(203) 566-5717

Florida

Department of Agriculture and Consumer Services
Mayo Building
Tallahassee FL 32301
(904) 488-2221

Georgia

Office of Consumer Affairs
#2 Martin Luther King Dr.
Plaza Level, East Tower
Atlanta GA 30334
(404) 656-3794

Idaho

Attorney General's Office
Business Regulation Division
Boise ID 83720
(208) 334-2400

Indiana

Consumer Protection Div.
Attorney General's Office
219 State House
Indianapolis IN 46204
(317) 232-6330

Iowa

Securities Division
Lucas State Office Building
Des Moines IA 50319
(515) 281-4441

Kentucky

Attorney General's Office
Consumer Protection Division
201 St. Clair
Frankfort KY 40601
(502) 564-2200

Louisiana

Department of Urban and Community Affairs
Consumer Protection Office
2610-A Woodale Blvd.
Baton Rouge LA 70804
(504) 925-4401

Maine

Department of Business Regulations
State House—Station 35
Augusta ME 04333
(207) 289-3915

Maryland

Office of the Attorney General
Securities Division
7 N. Calvert Street
Baltimore MD 21202
(301) 576-6360

Minnesota

Department of Commerce
Securities and Real Estate Division
5th Floor, Metro Square Building
7th & Roberts
St. Paul MN 55101
(612) 296-5689

Nebraska

Department of Banking and Finance
P.O. Box 95006
Lincoln NE 68509
(402) 471-2171

New Hampshire

Attorney General
Consumer Protection
State House Annex
Concord NH 03301
(603) 271-3641

North Carolina

Department of Justice
Consumer Protection Division
P. O. Box 629
Raleigh NC 27602
(919) 733-7741

Ohio

Attorney General
Consumer Fraud and Crime Section
15th Floor, State Office Tower
30 East Broad Street
Columbus OH 43215
(614) 466-8831

South Carolina

Office of the Secretary of State
Securities Division
816 Kennan Building
Columbia SC 29201
(803) 758-2833

Texas

Office of the Secretary of State
Uniform Commercial Code Division
P.O. Box 13193
Austin TX 78711
(512) 475-1769

Utah

Consumer Protection Division
160 East 300 South
Salt Lake City UT 84111
(801) 533-6601

Virginia

Consumer Affairs
1100 Bank Street
Richmond VA 23209
(804) 786-2042
(800) 552-9963

Washington

Department of Licensing
Securities Division
Highway License Building
12th and Franklin Streets
Olympia WA 98504
(206) 753-6928

17

To Join or Not to Join

Associations That Will Benefit You

Happiness is knowing someone cares.

In this world of bureaucracy, results come from the power of numbers. This is also where help comes from, usually in the least expensive way. Joining various groups can bring sizable benefits.

You have the local Chamber of Commerce, the Better Business Bureau, and probably a local or state chapter of whatever type industry you are in. Then there are the regional and/or national organizations.

It is impractical to think you could or would join every organization that exists, but there are two associations that should be paramount on your list. One is the national association of whatever industry you are involved in; the other is the International Franchise Association (IFA).

HOW THE INTERNATIONAL FRANCHISE ASSOCIATION CAN HELP

Your industry trade association will assist in keeping you abreast of product and/or service knowledge. The IFA will keep you informed on franchising in general. To be more specific, the IFA is a nonprofit trade association representing the major franchisors in the United States and around the world. It is the recognized spokesman for responsible franchising. The IFA was founded in 1960 by franchising executives who saw the need for an organization that would speak on behalf of franchising, provide services to member companies and those interested in franchising, set standards of business practice, serve as a medium of exchange of experience and expertise, and offer educational programs for franchisor management personnel. There are several categories of membership available. The IFA membership director may be contacted at the executive offices at 1350 New York Avenue NW, Suite 900, Washington, DC 20005 (202) 628-8000.

The Code of Ethics to which members in IFA subscribe is as follows:

I.   In the advertisement and grant of franchises or dealerships a member shall comply with all applicable laws and regulations and the member's offering circulars shall be complete, accurate and not misleading with respect to the franchisee's or dealer's investment, the obligations of the member and the franchisee or dealer under the franchise or dealership and all material facts relating to the franchise or dealership.

II. All matters material to the member's franchise or dealership shall be contained in one or more written agreements, which shall clearly set forth the terms of the relationship and the respective rights and obligations of the parties.

III. A member shall select and accept only those franchisees or dealers who, upon reasonable investigation, appear to possess the basic skills, education, experience, personal characteristics and financial resources requisite to conduct the franchised business or dealership and meet the obligations of the franchisee or dealer under the franchise and other agreements. There shall be no discrimination in the granting of franchises based solely on race, color, religion, national origin or sex. However, this in no way prohibits a franchisor from granting franchises to prospective franchisees as part of a program to make franchises available to persons lacking the capital, training, business experience, or other qualifications ordinarily required of franchisees or any other affirmative action program adopted by the franchisor.

IV. A member shall provide reasonable guidance to its franchisees or dealers in a manner consistent with its franchise agreement.

V.   Fairness shall characterize all dealings between a member and its franchisees or dealers. A member shall make every good faith effort to resolve complaints by and disputes with its franchisees or dealers through direct communication and negotiation. To the extent reasonably appropriate in the circumstances, a member shall give its franchisee or dealer notice of, and a reasonable opportunity to cure, a breach of their contractual relationship.

VI. No member shall engage in the pyramid system of distribution. A pyramid is a system wherein a buyer's future compensation is expected to be based primarily upon recruitment of new participants, rather than upon the sale of products or services.

18

Syndicate, Merge, Sell, Go Public or What?

Why You Need to Think About Structuring Your Company Now

One should buy stock when it is cheap. Wait for it to go up and then sell. If it does not go up, don't buy it.

There is a game often played in business which I call Egyptian football. The philosophy behind it is simple: When the ball is in the air, the rules may change.

With this in mind, I always like to have my companies and those of my clients in position to adapt no matter how the rules may change. Not knowing your company or your personal desires, I cannot suggest a course of direct action with regard to merger, acquisitions, selling out, or going public. I can, however, give you some guidelines in general areas.

THE FOUR BASICS FOR GOING PUBLIC OR SELLING OUT

Not long ago, one of our leading universities was holding a seminar entitled Going Public. I had the privilege of being invited to the seminar to lecture the class of about 200 attorneys and CPAs. There were numerous technical aspects covered; however, from management's point of view, there were basically only four principle items. First, get set up and start preparing three years ahead, if possible. Second, have someone beside you

79

as a guide who has done it for himself. Third, use professionals who have exact experience in the legal, accounting, and underwriting fields of going public. Fourth, be sure you really know your goals for now and the future.

These four items often apply also to selling or merging. Many of the principles are related, if not exactly alike. For this reason, I shall continue to explain the four points:

1. While I say prepare three years ahead, I really mean start now. That may sound like Egyptian football to you at this moment. You may not have the slightest inclination to go public or merge. On the other hand, the rules often change as time goes on. Sickness, competition, economic conditions, age, or any number of factors could cause a change in your rules, so why not prepare now? Basically, it costs no more to have your accounting, your board minutes, and your reporting policies all set up to meet the possible future criteria. It is just a matter of knowing how, with an eye toward the future, so it does not cost you anything extra to backtrack. It would cost a lot more to go back several years and do a cleanup.

2. The benefits of having someone beside you who has done it for himself are endless. Put that person on a flat fee for advice only. He need not perform any function other than advising; in fact, it is best that this be his only function. When you begin to think seriously about going public, selling, or merging, he should be placed under contract and paid whether you decide to take that action or not. This way he has only your interest at heart. He may really earn his money and do you a great service by suggesting "no go" on a deal.

Recently I was going over the costs and involvements of a small company that had gone public. If someone had been serving them as a knowledgeable advisor, they would probably have saved themselves 20 percent of their entire underwriting. Though they had gone public several years before, they still seemed happy with what had taken place. Ignorance is bliss, but it still cost them hundreds of thousands of dollars on this small offering, which was under $2 million.

3. Using professionals in the legal, accounting, and underwriting fields is another way of saving a great deal, not just in money, but in time, tension, and heartache. Knowing a professional who is sharp, fair, careful, and priced right is something special. You have to know all the right questions to find this type of person. It is important and it takes time, perhaps several months to get everyone lined up who will be right for your situation.

4. Being sure you know what your goals are is like asking you to look into an infallible crystal ball. Here again, the answers are not as important as knowing all the right questions. To sell out, merge, or go public may sound like a beautiful dream, but be sure. There are a number of personal desires, motivations, and dreams that must be dealt with as well as hard, cold business facts. Likewise, these business facts are not always what they seem on the surface or may not be as real tomorrow as they seem today.

I apologize for being so general in this chapter, but the subject is personal to each business. It is like one of those old "good-news, bad-news" stories: There were two partners who were on the acquisition trail. One partner visited a company in the Midwest that was for sale. He called his partner back home and said, "I've got some good news and some bad news. The good news is, instead of $17 million, they have agreed to take $15 million for the company. The bad news is they want $5,000 down."

Each situation is different and personal. It must be viewed by asking all the right questions. That is more important toward doing what is right for you than knowing the answers.

19

Laying Out a Franchise Agreement

Seventy-Seven Things You Need to Consider for Your Franchise Contract

A wedding is an event, but a marriage is an achievement.

In Chapter 12 I described the two types of contracts, the legal contract and the implied contract of human relations. I will now discuss the legal contract in more depth. The real attempt is to make the marriage of the two types hold together nicely without binding it so tightly there is a divorce under the strain.

As I have worked with franchisors who are new to the business, I am convinced more than ever that people who love sausage and those who design franchise agreements should never watch either one being made. This is especially true when an unseasoned franchise attorney or executive starts laying out a new franchise agreement. They either give away the store, open themselves to all types of future legal problems, or become overprotective and zealous in their undertaking. Sometimes they commit all three errors.

Presuming you know generally what you want to accomplish, the first step is to itemize the various things you as a franchisor will provide.

HERE IS YOUR GOAL

Next, you itemize what the franchisee will do. As you think through these rough ideas, there is a key philosophy which must be etched into the foreheads of everyone participating: "For me to be as successful as possible, my franchisees must be as successful as possible. I will not do anything to hinder this success process for either of us. Instead, I will do everything possible to enhance this process." Now that sounds elementary, yet you would be amazed at the reactions I get when I ask why someone wants a certain item put into a franchise agreement. Likewise, it is equally surprising to see how much can be taken out when it comes right down to "Do you really need this?" or "Is it worth the trouble or objections it will cause?"

HOW TO PROJECT TWENTY YEARS AHEAD

The next move is to put together a rough outline from your itemizations above. Acquiring an experienced consultant should follow. I know of no other way to arrive at the answers you need, which can be reached only by time and experience in the business. These answers are found through a consultant's conglomerate knowledge of sales, legal, accounting, marketing, and company capabilities. The questions are: How will all these things be accepted by the potential franchisee? How can the company perform these things? and What can we guess will be the franchisee reactions five, ten, or twenty years ahead as this franchise agreement continues? Only someone with a history in franchising can give the best answers.

Those who have learned lessons from the past have the best chance of not having to relive the expensive, time-consuming and perhaps fatal lessons in the future. A franchise license is more of a futuristic agreement than most contracts. It takes experience to lay it out realistically.

WHAT YOUR LOCAL ATTORNEY SHOULD DO

Next comes your local corporate counsel. He takes your outlines and, together with other information presumably supplied by the consultant, he forms the agreement. Here again, be careful. Your attorney is possibly a trusted friend and advisor, but you are coming to him for legal advice, not business advice.

I remember some years ago when our outside corporate counsel was new with us. One day, we all were in a meeting. A particular question was raised, and I asked counsel what he thought. His answer was, "I do not believe that is a legal decision. It seems to be more in the area of business management. If you are asking my opinion as a person, I will be glad to comment; but if you are asking me as your attorney, I think I should not comment." I immediately knew we had chosen a wise lawyer. Many years and many deals later, we have been proven right. The same holds true for your CPA. Accounting and taxes are his areas, not business management.

WHEN TO BRING IN THE FRANCHISE LEGAL SPECIALIST

When the corporate counsel has rough-typed the agreement, it should then go to a franchise attorney. This is extremely important. There are few specialists in this field, and minor points can put you out of business in years to come. The area of franchise law and regulations is not the same as general law. Do not treat it as such.

The franchise legal specialist will make any necessary changes to keep you safe and will corroborate same with your corporate counsel. Pride of authorship (ego) must take a backseat to the realization that having it right is paramount. Agreements that are unlawful may be chained to injunctions; they may cost large sums in damages. It has to be right. The basic, commonsense guidelines for the agreement are not that tough. First, the agreement should be in plain language, with full and complete disclosure in connection with the proposed relationship between the franchisor and franchisee. It should be so clear that later neither one can say they were unaware or deceived. Second, it should be fair in both directions. Neither side should be able to say they were coerced or lorded over by the other. Last, it should be a valid contract, enforceable by either party. They both should know what the consequences are if they breach anything promised in the agreement.

SEVENTY-SEVEN ITEMS TO CONSIDER IN YOUR FRANCHISE AGREEMENT

In general, the following are items you may want to cover in your franchise agreement:

1. What business are you in?
2. What business are you licensing?
3. Is there a territory involved?
4. Are there exclusive rights?

5. Is there new construction involved or conversion of existing structures?
6. What is the initial licensee fee?
7. What is the royalty fee?
8. What is the product sold or service performed?
9. Who is your franchisee contact person or key person?
10. What are the standards and specifications for controls?
11. Is there pro forma assistance for loan applications?
12. Will you assist in preparing a loan package?
13. Do you make loans or participate in loans?
14. Is there franchise owner orientation training?
15. Is there manager operator training?
16. Is there continued training?
17. What manuals are furnished?
18. Is there grand opening assistance?
19. What are your practices with regard to sale of supplies, furniture, and equipment?
20. Inspection criteria
21. Advertising requirements and participation
22. In-house publications for franchisee's edification
23. Bookkeeping and accounting assistance
24. Chart of accounts to be furnished
25. Consulting assistance
26. Recommendations and assistance in regard to franchisee associations or advisory councils
27. Complete outline of system standards
28. Licensing of what trademarks and trade names
29. Assistance regarding construction, conversion, etc.
30. Furnishing of plans and specifications
31. Number and type of inspections
32. Explanation of various technical terms
33. Accounting and reporting methods
34. Forms to be used
35. Periods to be used for accounting
36. Payment requirements
37. Penalties for delinquencies

38. Record retention requirements
39. Discounts for multiple-unit owners
40. Reduced royalties for distressed situations
41. System advertising and charges
42. Authorization for dissemination of confidential information
43. Insurance and indemnity requirements
44. Condemnation, destruction, and reconstruction requirements
45. Conditions upon desired sale of franchised business
46. First rights of refusal
47. Types of ownership permitted
48. Arbitration
49. Transfer of license fees
50. Conditions of termination
51. Responsibilities after termination
52. Transfer upon death
53. Options in event of default
54. Method of giving notices
55. Severability
56. Relationship of the parties
57. Disclaimer statements
58. Rights of inheritance
59. Renewal options
60. Liquidating damages
61. Maintenance requirements
62. Renovation requirements
63. Standards for supplies
64. Operating hours of business
65. Marketing assistance
66. Inspection of franchisee records
67. Notification of other business activities
68. Right of assignment by franchisor
69. Terms of leases
70. Minimum volume required
71. Display requirements in unit
72. Display requirements in local market area

73. Service facility requirements
74. Credit relations
75. Inventory requirements
76. Decor requirements
77. Future name changes

You may decide to have an application prior to the franchise agreement. If so, some of the items to consider would be:

1. Information desired on the applicant
2. Must have a location or is it to be acquired?
3. Various disclaimers
4. His evaluation of qualifications of the franchise opportunity
5. Time period for him to evaluate the potential franchise
6. Feasibility requirements
7. Accept individuals only or other entities?
8. Scope of your application approval policies
9. Time period to evaluate application approval

The franchise agreement, as you can see, can grow to many pages. Just be sure that after all is said and done, you are not guilty of much being said and little being done.

20

Establishing Fees

What They Are and How Much They Should Be

The amount of sleep required by the average person is just five minutes more.

Like that five minutes more of sleep, the average person wants just a little more when it comes to setting fees for himself. The reverse is true of the one doing the paying.

Probably one of the most delicate areas is determining what a fair, profitable, competitive, and saleable initial franchise and continuing royalty fee should be. Likewise, it is hard for a company just beginning to measure the cost of services to be performed for the franchisee and the standard franchisor backup costs. It is especially difficult when you must project into the future for five, ten, or twenty years.

There are usually industry norms for fees and the advertising fund contributions. This does not mean these norms are correct for you. In fact, I personally dislike doing things like everyone else. I believe the unique, the different, is the route to great fortunes which are still untapped.

So what do you charge, you with your "I do it different from everyone else in the industry business"? Again, this is where someone with experience comes in. It will take some psychology of the marketplace and experience with franchisor costs to help you.

FEES IN RELATION TO VALUE

The fee should have a relationship to the value received. You may have to show a value breakdown should you ever have a court test by someone.

Naturally, your name and so on has worth, which will undoubtedly increase as your system becomes more successful and better known. The allocation for your portion of value will probably increase your initial franchise/license fee over the years as well. Then there are the other services—for example, perhaps site selection assistance, training, plans and specifications, accounting systems, manuals provided, grand opening assistance, and the like. All of these and others may or may not be programmed into your initial fee.

Next comes the continuing royalty, if that is your method of operation. Should you have a distribution type of franchise, your fee would possibly be built into the product cost to the franchise/dealer. If you use a percentage of gross sales as a royalty fee, there must be some fine-tuning of your accounting pencil. Costs for a new operation are often hard to project, however, they are not impossible to estimate by any means. There are competition factors and future dollar evaluations that should be projected also. It is complicated, and you must be fairly accurate since this item is probably your largest future income stream.

HOW TO ACCOUNT FOR THE FEES

You need to consider the consequences of the services performed or to be performed behind the initial franchise/license fee. Just what effect will these services have or when do you want to put that fee into your income for profit-and-loss benefits? There are legal and accounting practices of which you must be cognizant. Usually there are three primary methods. One would be to spread the fee over the life of your franchise agreement. As you can see, this would allow you to show only a small portion each year. If the term is not defined exactly for a specific number of years, this could be a problem.

Another method of putting the fee into income would start when the initial rights and services begin or at the actual inception of the relationship as an operating unit. This has some problems also if preopening services are performed for the franchisee.

The third method would be the cash method. When you get it, you show it. This is probably the weakest method of all, since you would usually receive all or a portion of the fee prior to the franchisee beginning operation. It would probably be considered "not earned" at that point.

In general terms, your CPA will probably say the revenue can be recognized when the sale is concluded by substantial performance of the initial sale and completion of start-up services promised. That usually means when the franchisee goes "on line" as a fully operating unit.

There are important tax consequences of when these fees are "booked." Careful planning should be made in advance. One does not just pick a figure and charge it.

CONSIDERATIONS REGARDING AREA OR MASTER FRANCHISES

Should you decide on area-type franchising where the area or master franchisee has the right to franchise in his area, other considerations come into play. Generally, with this type of operation there is a sizable up-front franchisee fee. Next are some of the same questions concerning when to recognize the income. If there are performance items for the franchisor, or if there is a refund basis, then recognition of income probably has to be delayed.

The income received for initial fees usually represents both tangible and intangible services on the part of the franchisor. It is, therefore, difficult to determine when the fee has been earned. The American Institute of Certified Public Accountants states, and the Securities Exchange Commission has widely accepted, the fact that in most cases performance is considered "substantially completed" with the franchisee becoming operational. We also must deal with the probability of collecting the fee in periodic payments. Perhaps non-interest-bearing notes for same and the possibility of repurchase of the franchise by the franchisor will come into play.

21

Qualification and Selection of the Proper Franchisees

How to Select Franchisees—A Critical Choice

Great people are just ordinary people with an extraordinary amount of determination.

One dreary, rainy morning I got on the elevator going to the tenth floor. On the elevator was a young delivery man, about twenty-five years old, with a small package. He was obviously feeling good, smiling and humming to himself. I looked over at him and said, "You seem rather happy on this rainy day." "Yes sir," he replied. "I ain't never lived this day before!" What a great attitude.

WHY THE INTERVIEWER/SALESPERSON IS IMPORTANT

I can list all the various cut-and-dried qualifications for choosing franchisees and then there is that nebulous one... of attitude. I'm sure we have all seen people who did great jobs even though the technical qualifications were lacking, because of attitude. When we set up rules for a screening process, one of the most important items is to have the person doing the interviews trained to recognize the value of the "human qualifications." This is sometimes a vague area we may refer to as gut reaction, intuition, and maybe just plain feelings. If you are not careful, these same feelings can also sway you into choosing the wrong people. It is extremely important that the interviewer/salesperson understand all this.

Several years back there was a young man I knew well who applied for a job as a sales representative with an international advertising agency. The position was available in one of our larger southern cities. This large corporation had numerous requirements, such as a minimum age of twenty-five, at least two years of college, and previous sales experience. There were others, but these were the ones this young man did not have. He was twenty-three years old, had no college and only limited sales experience. The local manager's secretary was handling the initial paper-work. She tried to discourage the young man from even filling out the application, but he politely insisted. She told him it was a waste of time because "rules were rules" and these requirements were in the hiring procedures manual. He persisted anyway, then asked to see the boss.

The local manager saw him out of courtesy, but said he couldn't change the rules. The young man wanted the job and proceeded to sell the manager on how good he would be for the company. The manager was impressed with this young man's logic and perseverance; he saw a desire and maturity he thought the company should consider. He set up a meeting with his superior. The following week, the young man went through the same procedure only to get the same answer, "I can't change the rules from the home office . . . but you do sound good." "Well," said the young man, "who does have the authority to hire me?" The boss was further impressed this man was not going to go down in defeat.

Next there was an appointment set up with the vice-president of the region. He had the power to lift the rules. The young man impressed him and was offered the job. He completed the corporation training school and by the end of the first year was in first or second place in the entire region every time the sales figures were published. At the age of twenty-seven he became the youngest district manager in the history of this worldwide corporation.

It is important to bend the rules occasionally and you need a sharp "bender" on your side to make that choice. Pay that interviewer/represent-ative well because his sales abilities and judgments may be one of your big assets.

Now let's get to some of the more structured dos and don'ts. Since you have read the preceding chapters, you know reasons why businesses fail. Go back to Chapter 9 and pick out the points that apply to your screening process for franchisees. In the old days, some new companies in franchising would sell to anyone who was warm and had the money. Today it is a much more serious transaction. Experience has taught that a failure with your trade-name sign out front can do a lot of damage. In addition, today you must report failures and/or terminations in some disclosure documents that are given to potential franchisees. It just seems natural that when reading about several of these in your offering documents, a potential franchisee would think, "That could be me." That certainly might be the very thought that kills your sales.

HOW TO BUILD A PSYCHOLOGICAL PROFILE

Depending on the type of franchise you are selling, you may want to do a psychological work-up on your potential franchisee. Several colleges and universities or industrial psychologists can supply you with simplified tests. They are or can be designed to tell you many things about the ability, education, adaptability, fears, desire, and general possibilities for success in your type of endeavor. This may not be too important if your franchise opportunity is one in which the franchisee is simply a passive investor who has someone else managing for him. On the other hand, if it is a franchisee-operated business, it may be of real value to you.

A potential franchisee may have enough money to buy your deal, but without the other skills and desires you may have a new failure in the making. Carefully evaluating what is in a person's head is definitely as important as what comes out of his mouth. When you have several dozen operating franchises, you can do a profile on them. An evaluation of the successful profiles will tell you what to look for as you test your future applicants. Naturally, you choose only the ones who have the type of positive profile your successful operators show. Above all, stay away from those who show the traits of your unsuccessful operators.

Building this profile of psychological qualifications will save you a lot of time and money. You will then be expending your efforts on people who can succeed. It also reveals other factors. By knowing the type, caliber, education level, and so on of persons you are looking for, you now can choose where and how to spend best your advertising dollar to find them. This will not only save you money, but will make it for you, since you are courting the correct market segment.

HOW TO SCREEN THE POTENTIAL FRANCHISEE

If the potential franchisee is reasonably sharp, he should be impressed with how carefully you screen applicants. This should reassure him about investing his time, money, and perhaps life's work in your system. He can see you want to be positive that he is right for your system. You will have a successful franchise, which means he personally will be a success—all of which is what all parties want.

The screening process must always delve into the detailed financial ability of the potential franchisee. Be careful with this one. People in general overestimate their capital abilities. Just because he has purchased a car or two, a refrigerator, furniture, and house on credit may mean he is thinking of borrowing what it takes to get into your deal. Starting on all borrowed funds may spell capital shortage and failure should things not go exactly as planned. Get a full explanation of the potential franchisee's complete financial situation.

On the other hand, those who have acquired reasonable wealth may have unreal expectations of mortgage and finance possibilities. They may also have inflated their net worth statement in order to qualify for your deal.

What are the potential franchisee's desires for his life? Go beyond what he says. Hear the words that are unspoken. How does his past life script fit with what he says?

For an owner-operator potential franchisee, I think the ideal would be someone who is business-minded, independent, creative in his thought processes, and who wants to break out of the "working for someone else" mold. The investor franchisee is another type. Some systems will not consider a prospect unless he operates. Others will accept passive investors. It depends on your system and how it works best. Either way, a personal visit is necessary from an evaluation standpoint on both sides and necessary from a sales standpoint. Both parties can bring things to a head faster this way. It saves money for your company to proceed or conclude with a prospect as fast as possible.

22

Franchisor-Franchisee Relations

How to Build a Strong Franchisee Organization

*Good judgment comes from experi-
ence. Experience comes from bad
judgment.*

If we are smart enough to learn from someone else's experience, we do not
have to go through the expense of making bad judgments ourselves. We
call it "going to school on someone else."

I have seen the attitude of a franchisor take a viable company down
the tube to bankruptcy. As I mentioned in Chapter 19 with regard to
franchise agreements, the contract of human relations is probably the most
important one of all. Nothing can replace a straightforward, honest, above-
board approach in any human relationship. It builds trust and belief on the
other side. Isn't that what we are all seeking?

There are no secrets, regardless of what you think. Thinking there are
and attempting to live that life script personally or in business is not the
best way to go.

HOW TO LOSE FRANCHISEES

Some franchisors say things differently. They perceive the franchisee on
one side and them on the other. They say things like, "We are all one big
family" or "What is good for them is good for us." Yet their day-to-day
actions speak otherwise. That does not breed good relationships, but

instead perpetuates the opposite. It builds giant walls of distrust. If there is a problem, face it and say it. If something is good, face it and say it. The unsaid can often be damaging, or at least not achieve the benefits possible, merely because it was not said.

Some franchisors have a unique, big-buck idea or system that is presently strong, and they may operate on the theory that "a Smith and Wesson beats four aces." For a while that is possible, perhaps. In the end, the free enterprise system, the franchisees, the public, or the government will probably call their bluff. The challenge may even go so far as to put you out of business. I am not suggesting that you be benevolent or give away the farm. I am suggesting that good, well-planned, long-range business judgments be made with a great deal of "in-touch-with-the-world/ marketplace" realism.

An additional cause of franchisee unrest is just plain craziness on their part. There are some people who will never be happy no matter what you do. The secret is for you to be able to judge accurately who is unreasonable and who isn't. I am quite familiar with two particular franchisees who are this way. They are making money with their franchise, but at the same time, they would not be pleased even if the franchisor offered them everything free.

Recently I was asked to testify before a Senate subcommittee in connection with a strange bill that had been backed by some unhappy franchisees. During the hearings, the committee chairman asked one of the franchisees what he was worth when he started his first franchise. He stated he had $25,000. The chairman then asked him what his current net worth was and how many franchises he now owned. He answered by saying he had twenty-six outlets and was worth over two million dollars. "Why," said the chairman, "are you now trying to get more out of the franchisor? It looks like they have been pretty profitiable for you." The franchisee thought for a moment and then said, "I guess I'm just greedy." His franchisor was sitting next to me and said he had a copy of the franchisee's last financial statement. It showed his net worth currently as $25 million.

It is almost impossible to work with some people/franchisees. Thank heavens they are in a very, very small minority; however, this is again all the more reason for choosing your franchisees carefully.

HOW TO GROW FRANCHISEES

If we were to attempt to classify what franchisor-franchisee relations are, we would have to use words like *profit, opportunity, psychic remunerations, motivation, rapport, desires, purpose*—all the things we all have to consider for our franchisor organizations.

That being the case, then, there is one big thing to set up as a prime thought: A candle loses nothing by lighting another candle. At the same time, we all gain more light when that happens. When our thoughts can revolve around assisting the franchisee to be a success, then we are using our candle to light another. And we have gained.

At this point, the franchisee is a believer. He has bought your methods and ideas; he is gung ho on your program. But beware of the franchisees who within a short time become "experts" and think they are smarter than you. Thereafter comes the challenge. Generally if you have assisted them properly and they are operating profitably, they will be behind you.

The best beginning of any relationship comes from truth. Never, never blue-sky your opportunity to him. Not only can you get into legal trouble, but you are cruising for a disappointed franchisee.

You must make the franchisee aware of his or her responsibilities in the relationship. Occasionally a franchisee thinks everything should come from you. It is a business arrangement and the franchisor cannot do it all, nor can you afford to pay for everything. If that is the situation, say so.

In the beginning, you should outline exactly what you will and, above all, will not do. Have it in writing. Have the franchisee go over it two or three times. Some companies put this on tape or film and play it for the franchisee, give it to him or her in writing, and have him or her sign for it as well. Be sure you can deliver what you have promised. This first step is vitally important to the mutual understanding of the relationship.

Earlier I used the phrase "psychic remuneration." That refers to the reward you get from you own head by feeling good/okay. *Psychology Today* magazine did a cross-country survey recently and found that a very high percentage of people are unhappy with their position in life or their job. One of the key factors is the lack of recognition, respect, and consideration they receive from their superiors. This is not a money reward they seek. It is psychic recognition. It is the same with all of us, and that includes franchisees.

Awards to franchisees, their managers, and others are very important. Trophies, photos, recognition from in-house publications, from the platform at meetings, and so on all produce good results. Listening and reacting to their ideas are especially important. Just be sure your recognition/reaction is real. Do not trump up something or it will backfire with others in your organization, as well as the franchisees, who can see the truth.

Expansion possibilities can serve as another reward for the franchisee and franchisor. It is a good way to stimulate self-motivation. Ego and/or money may both be factors. As a franchisee becomes successful, his potential is increased economically and managerially. His desire is usually increased also.

HOW TO COMMUNICATE WITH FRANCHISEES

If I mention the word *communication,* you immediately think, "I know that already." I'm sure you do. The "how to get through" is another problem we all have, and that is part of what makes up communication. We can publish a certain piece of information in monthly house organs, send out operations bulletins, have the inspector in the field tell each franchisee, and announce it at the regional meeting. Six months later some franchisees will tell you they never heard of it. This is an age-old problem. The solutions are discussed at every franchisor meeting I have ever attended. Entire workshops have been held on the subject. There is no pat answer. Some things work better for some franchisors than others. In trying to solve this problem for your company, you should give serious consideration to the general education and interest level of your franchisees. As one correlates this type of information, one can decide how better to communicate.

HOW TO ORGANIZE A FRANCHISEE ASSOCIATION

One of the best communication methods developed is the franchisee association or council. I have a switch for an old saw: "You can lead a horse to water, but if you can get him to float on his back, you have really done something." Teaching—helping franchisees to float on their backs—is a tough trick. One of the best ways I know to accomplish this is through peer teaching. Why? Because humans seem to trust and believe their peers faster and in more depth. In addition, belonging and being a believing, striving part gives each participant a big boost. Then there are all the other psychological reasons for peer following. We see it yearly as the styles in clothes change. We experienced it strongly in our teenage years. We see the power of it in our teenagers today. Peer influence can be implemented effectively through a franchisee association or council.

Now you are horrified. Help the franchisees form an organization for unification? Help them form a union against you? I can make only one comment: They will form some type of organization. It will happen. So it seems better to start with you steering it than without your guidance. People are smart; they understand more than often given credit for. It won't take long before some unreasonable franchisee who wants some ego glory decides on an issue and attempts to organize the rest of your franchisees, with him as president. Or perhaps it is a reasonable franchisee who starts it just to improve his lot. Stay a leader—start the ball rolling, help put the bylaws in order, and see that rational franchisees are installed with you sitting beside them. Now you and the rational franchisees can gradually teach those other "horses," who are helping you pull the load to "float on their backs."

In your franchise agreement, you may want to state that a majority vote of the franchisee association or its executive committee may be considered an affirmative approval of all franchisees. This can become a simplified method of handling a vastly complicated procedure of bringing about changes.

Probably one of the greatest assets of our company's franchisee association is the sharing of ideas. The dynamic nature of each franchisee entrepreneur is not to be underestimated. If you want to know as much as possible about the problems in your system, go to the person who has one and lives with it daily—your franchisee. If you want new solutions and perhaps creative new ideas, go to the same person. It is amazing how much money can be saved or made through this method of communication. It is also amazing how much good will and cooperation you will build by this type of sharing.

Our company was so pleased with this method that we created seats on our board of directors for nominees from the franchisee association. They are extremely proud and protective of those seats. Both sides have now become one side. When people are on the inside and see the reasons for things, rarely do they disagree. In addition, they convey this feeling to the other franchisees. They have a forum in which they can be heard legitimately. We have the same. It functions so well that generally we process a major change first through the association executive committee people. They help us refine it and then we both present it to all the franchisees.

We have placed two franchisees on the licensing committee and two on the unified advertising committee. It works extremely well. Rational people striving together for a common goal—sounds like the democratic, free enterprise system to me.

Caution! If your purpose in forming a franchisee association is to control your franchisees, to make them all think exactly as you do, you are headed for trouble. That is the wrong purpose. Remember how you qualified these people before you let them join your system? They are not dumb, unaggressive pushovers. They are smart, aggressive people. That is why you chose them. If your purpose is to assist in communications, to maximize profits, obtain pleasure from accomplishments, and so on, then you are on the right horse.

I must add that there are always exceptions. Occasionally there are companies who possibly would not benefit greatly from an association or council of franchisees. These companies, however, are not the norm.

Associations come about in various ways. There are three ways they usually are created:

1. The franchisor appoints members, sets the meeting dates, and runs the meeting.
2. The franchisees meet and organize everything for themselves. Later, they may invite the franchisor to participate to some extent.
3. The franchisor and franchisee jointly put things together, sharing the responsibilities.

HOW TO WRITE THE BYLAWS FOR YOUR FRANCHISEE ASSOCIATION

The bylaws of the association can range from fully incorporated organizations to just a general set of rules. Usually, either will contain at least the following:

1. Who can belong
2. Who can be an officer or director
3. Where the meeting will be held
4. When the meeting will be held
5. Who pays for what
6. Who will conduct the meetings
7. Who or how many must be present for a quorum
8. Who has what responsibilities
9. Who will do the paperwork for the association

Since times and truths change, be sure the bylaws contain provisions for making changes in the future. Make the mechanics safe yet uncumbersome.

Membership is usually affected by one of two methods. Members may be appointed by the franchisor, but most often they are elected by their peers.

Formal leadership is a must, otherwise your channel of communications and function performance breaks down. They need to be specific as to:

1. Number of officers
2. How they are elected
3. How long they serve
4. What exactly are their duties

Usually the officers are elected by their peers, but it is not uncommon for the franchisor to appoint them, or sometimes there is a combination of the two methods.

There are four areas in which the association is usually involved on committees:

1. Operations
2. Services
3. Marketing
4. Finance

The agenda for a meeting will cover one or all of the committee areas and special items of concern. It is ideal to have a cooperative effort between the executive committee of the association and the franchisor toward an agenda.

As the association matures, advisory committees comprised of past presidents often will emerge. Their main function is usually "level-headed thinking" based on past experiences. Often they function in areas of bylaw changes, assisting committees, special projects, and important technical changes between franchisees and franchisors.

HOW FRANCHISORS SHOULD PARTICIPATE

The amount of participation by the franchisor varies according to the association. No matter what the amount of involvement, it is imperative that only the very top level of management be included. To have lower management or even vice presidents participate (unless they are senior or executive V.P.'s) is usually unwise. This is an important area and must be watched closely. If a discussion is to involve operations, perhaps you will want to have the V.P. of operations with you at the meeting, but the top people definitely should be involved if all we are outlining is to be accomplished.

There are several ways of handling expenses for these meetings. The most common is for the franchisor to cover the cost of the facilities for the meeting and maybe even the cost of some or all of the meals. Generally the association or the individuals will cover the cost of travel and lodging. Some associations set fixed dues, some are supported by the franchisor, and some are a combination of both. The dues method is probably the most popular.

As a franchisor, always remember to follow up and report progress to your franchisee association. When they make suggestions, if you plan on letting matters slide, say so! Do not agree to do something and then drop it; you will lose credibility fast. Besides, this is playing games. If that is the way you think and act, you are not being honest—even with yourself—and it will come back to haunt you. If you do agree to try something, then report back continually so the association will know what is going on. They will learn to have faith in you, thus improving your relationship. Follow through and report back. Both are extremely important tools of good management.

Since there can be legal situations that arise in connection with associations, it is advisable to have an attorney involved when the bylaws are being formalized. He should be especially versed in the areas of the Sherman Antitrust and Robinson-Patman acts. There should never be any discussions concerning prices, who will or will not be getting a franchise, or the exclusion of anyone from the association without just cause. These are dangerous areas.

DOS AND DON'TS OF FRANCHISEE ASSOCIATIONS

A survey of the members of IFA who have franchisee associations/councils reveal some recommended dos and don'ts. Generally they summarize as follows:

1. Do have a written set of bylaws or a constitution.
2. Don't consider the bylaws unchangeable. Include provisions for same.

3. Do set broad goals and objectives from the very beginning.

4. Don't limit attendance to just franchise owners and top management. Pull in key people for specific topics.

5. Do have someone responsible for taking notes at meetings and distributing same.

6. Don't let the national association/council get bogged down with items or duties that can be handled by a regional council group. Spread the work load to involve people, but spread it to the proper levels.

7. Do set an agenda for each meeting and stick to it. If you don't, the meetings can often turn into gripe sessions.

8. Don't waste the experience of your association's past presidents. Use them for special tasks.

9. Do have the franchisor's top management people at the meetings.

10. Don't invite hassles over who pays for what in connection with the association and franchisor activities. Decide in advance. This gives the association a reputation as an effective organization.

11. Do have a follow-up method of keeping the members informed of the association and franchisor activities.

12. Don't create legal problems. Be aware of the implications and unified actions an association can have.

There are various levels of an association. Much depends on how large you are in numbers, as well as how you are spread geographically. You might have an international association made up of franchise members who are the presidents of your franchisee associations from various nations. You might have regional associations that comprise the various areas of the particular country. Their presidents may sit on the board of your national association.

The activities scope, as well as the bylaws, are so varied that it would be cumbersome to try to outline them here. I have accumulated information on various associations over the years and found that although the ideas, purposes, and goals differ greatly, all are similar in many basic ways.

The following are answers to questions I am often asked about associations:

1. Most meet quarterly.

2. The association's officers/delegates are most often selected by the franchisees.

3. Most franchisors pay the cost of delegates attending the meetings.

4. Each delegate usually serves two or three years.

5. Most often the franchisor calls the meetings.

6. Most franchisors feel the association has been helpful in improving communications and relations.

7. The areas that the association has been of most assistance are in operations and positive relations toward the franchisors.

23

Communication Is Everything

How to Get Things Done the Way You Want

> *Waiter: "How did you find the meat, sir?"*
> *Customer: "I just lifted the potato chip and there it was."*

In this case, the question the waiter had in his mind was not the question the customer heard. Even between people who know each other very well, at times there are misunderstandings of the spoken word.

Sometimes written communication is even worse. Branches of government and home offices are especially bad in this area. They spew out volcanoes of Jell-O. Have you ever read a memo, reread the memo, then carefully begun to read it a third time, marking it sentence by sentence because it was just plain confusing? Now you know what I'm saying.

THE SIMPLE ELEMENTS OF COMMUNICATING EFFECTIVELY

To communicate effectively, we must be aware of what I call the S-D-R formula. The *S* is for sending. We must be conscious of the words we use so we can be sure the receiver Decodes (the *D*) as we meant him to do. This is necessary so the Reaction (the *R*) will be what we desire.

When lecturing at seminars on communication, I often ask the class if they know what the emergency distress signal SOS stands for. I get answers like "Save our souls" and "Save our ship." The truth is, it does not stand for anything. It was devised to meet the same criteria I have adopted in my S-D-R formula. A signal was needed that could be sent by Morse code, one that was easy to remember and "Send" quickly. It had to be simple to "Decode." The underlying desire was the ability to get the correct "Reaction," because the saving of life or property was at stake. Thus, S-D-R.

The ability to be honest in our communications is a psychological learning process. Being direct and to the point without being offensive is the goal of that process. We can add a basic problem to the process: The franchisor and the franchisee do not have the same business philosophy, nor do they speak the same language. We might say they are at crossed purposes in some areas.

The management of the franchisor company is usually symbolized as having a growth psychology. The typical franchisee is not as motivated in this direction. The franchisee is not usually the type of person who would struggle to the top of large corporate managment, which would be typical of the franchisor. Generally, the franchisee could be characterized as a psychologically semi-static type of personality. The typical franchisor in top management is someone who probably sets high goals relative to income, status, and power. The usual franchisee would more likely have moderate goals in those areas.

WATCH YOUR TECHNICAL LANGUAGE

Our very language in technical spheres is also different. We use buzzwords and phrases that are peculiar to our business as a franchisor; they may be foreign to the average franchisee. This is true in all industries, and is often fostered because it allows members of a profession to feel they belong to the "in group."

The average franchisee would comprehend the following words, but not necessarily in the context used by the franchisor:

1. Profit margin
2. Automation
3. Marketing
4. Staff functions
5. Life functions
6. Regional expansion
7. Executive dynamics
8. Field inspector coordination

WHY NEVER TO ASSUME ABOUT DESIRES

What do we do about all this? First, we never assume that the desires or goals of the franchisee are the same as ours. Our obligation is to find out what are his basic life desires or goals. How does his operation of a franchise fit into this pattern? A franchisee's goals often change after a few years. If this happens, you must be aware of this change in order to continue to communicate effectively.

In your communication awareness, be conscious of the nonverbal transactions. These can tell you a lot about a franchisee's attitude and viewpoint. Does he try to bring your meeting to an end by rushing things? Does he clam up and give you the silent treatment? Does he initiate spurts of letter writing on subjects that are not as important as the writer seems to think? Are meetings prolonged or disorganized? Is he late or perhaps doesn't show up at all? Is he paying attention to the conversation or is his mind wandering? Is he early for meetings? The list could go on and on.

HOW NEVER TO BE CAUGHT OFF GUARD

Another important item for successful communications is preplanning. If we contact our operations inspectors or other department heads, we usually can find out how a franchisee is thinking. Rarely do we ever have to be taken by surprise. I call it my "Quick Draw McGraw" technique. Anticipate the situation. Check with others for information. Next, be fast on the draw. Since you have checked up and found the possible problems or good situations in advance, you can now formulate your thoughts or answers when the franchisee hits you with a problem or question.

Last, be direct. Be sure of what you know and feel. Commmunicate it honestly and directly. Do not pussyfoot around, evade, or allude to the situation. Hit it straight. Your chances of success are much, much better this way.

HOW TO TEACH YOUR EMPLOYEES TO UNDERSTAND

Empathy is another factor toward great success. If you have not walked in the franchisee's moccasins, you cannot totally understand his point of view. If you have not suffered the slings and arrows of being a franchisee, you cannot understand his reasoning accurately. To be able to feel and understand brings amazing results.

A few years back, I decided some of our home-office people just were not shouldering or reacting enough to the burdens of franchisees. Yet they were intelligent people who understood their jobs. I decided that everyone who had not worked in one of our motels should do so. The vice president of operations scheduled each person in the motels for several days. The results were great. Thereafter, when a franchisee or his motel manager called in for something, or with a problem, the people taking the call understood him. They knew how he felt and comprehended the situation. They handled it with gusto. When someone called for the department head and he was out, the secretary asked if she could help. The franchisee, glad to get someone's attention, told her the situation. The secretary had worked in a motel and understood the problem. She would tell the franchisee she knew who to go to for the answer. She did, got the answer, and called him back. There was no aggravating delay and the department head was not bothered. Walk in those moccasins, gripe or handle gripes in them, and everyone will benefit.

It also can result in profits. After all our people from the mail driver to the president, worked at the motels, we held debriefing sessions. The profitable ideas that came from firsthand experiences saved and made us a lot of money, made our employees feel good, and received positive reactions from franchisees.

You can look at an apple for the first time, then you can describe it—but until you take a bite of it, you cannot truly describe the apple. To want people with knowledge is certainly desirable. To want hands-on experience and knowledge is more desirable, as well as profitable.

Remember in communications to "shishkebob" your conversations. Between the morsels of meat put some onion, peppers, or tomato. The meat is the facts. The onion, pepper, or tomato becomes the benefit. Never assume that because you have outlined the facts, the franchisee understands the benefits.

It is a fact that a watch has a nice gold band. The benefit is that you can keep it on your wrist with that band. You are not as likely to lose the watch, then, and the gold band is decorative and expensive looking. This adds possible status when some people see it on your wrist. You can call it selling, but it is a communication necessity. Never assume that franchisees understand the benefits, just because you have laid out the facts. This applies to almost everyone you have contact with.

Certainly one of the most effective methods of communications with franchisees is through the franchisee association or council. The advantages have already been covered; but I want to impress upon you once more the importance of this vehicle.

HOW TO SEEK SO YOU CAN FIND

Do not forget the great value of asking franchisees what they think, how they feel, and what suggestions they have. Just as you should never assume they understand, you should never assume you know as much as they do or know what they think. Ask! You will be amazed constantly at what you will learn that can make or save you and other franchisees a lot of money. You do not have a corner on brains. Everyone has some.

Recently, I gave a simple test to a group. I divided the meeting into six groups of about ten people each. I gave each person a list of fifteen items one might take on a spacecraft moon trip. I asked them to list priority numbers beside the items, starting with one and ending with fifteen. First I had each person prioritize the list individually. Then I had them do one sheet in each group. They were amazed when they graded their individual and group sheets against the correct answers. In every case, the individuals scored far below the group. This was because the group reasoned out the answers together. One person knew something about magnetism on the moon (one of the items on the list was a magnetic compass); another had read about something else. Together they had more answers right. So ask your employees, your franchisees, everyone, what they think.

Another benefit is morale. We all like to be consulted, to have input, to be respected for our ideas. Cooperation improves on all fronts. Profits improve because you now have more answers right than before. Absenteeism even goes down. So much can be learned if we will only listen to our people. This is especially true of line people who have direct contact with customers. We often do things that our clerks, salesmen, or outlet managers possibly could have told us would not work if we had just asked them. Often, the best profit we can make is the money we save by avoiding mistakes.

When we attempt to build model communications, we must remember it is like fertilizer. Too little doesn't help; too much burns up the crop. I know a real estate salesman who makes me feel uncomfortably sorry for him every time I'm around him. He is so overly lavish with his greeting, his "How are you," his "Glad to see you," his "I'd love to help you," and on and on. The "fertilizer" is so heavy and abnormal, I would be afraid to trust him. He seems insincere.

It would be nice if we did not have to take the time to fertilize, but the proper amount of fertilization is always worth the effort. For your company, as in farming, the question is not "do you or don't you," but "how much" and "when." Too little of the fertilizer of communications and people or plants will spread out their roots to seek more nourishing soil. Some wait too long to feritlize and the leaves start to turn brown. A sharp manager will not let a situation go too far before he steps up and communicates honestly. It is possible to overfertilize, also, just as some call too many meetings, require too many reports or too many details. They strangle their people by overdoing, going beyond the necessary. Don't overcommunicate; be realistic and practical.

HOW TO WRITE AND SPEAK TO GET ACTION

A study was made some years ago in a leading New England university with regard to levels of words that could be communicated to achieve the most understanding. It is a rating system called the Fog Index. While it goes into depth as to how to write or speak to gain this success, the bottom line is: Give it out so a sixth grader could understand it. The system is great, and it is easy to index your written communications. Probably you will be astounded.

Also look at your company's memos, bulletins, and any other information that goes to franchisees. Go find some secretary, clerk, or delivery driver, whoever is most likely to know the least about the subject in the bulletin. Ask them to read it and explain what they think it says, paragraph by paragraph. After trying this a few times, you may want to make some changes in the communications that go out of your office. Remember, you are not trying to impress anyone with polysyllabic words. The goals are S-D-R. And really it is only the R we are concerned with. You want the right Reaction on the receiver's end.

The primary spot to start with is that R. What is the ultimate goal you want from the receiver? Design from that point. Be careful not to run off at the pen. Go over the communications piece. Take a pencil and strike out every word, phrase, or sentence that could be left out, or replace three sentences with only one, worded differently but still producing the desired result.

Does anyone ever analyze the cost-benefit relationship of some of your regular reports or bulletins which go out or merely circulate in your office? Once I was doing a consulting job for a medium-sized franchisor. During a conversation, the vice president mentioned the high cost of paper and printing. From there, I designed a very simple check system. In fact, it was so simple it took me all of three minutes. I put it into action by merely placing it in the hands of every home office employee with a one-paragraph explanation attached.

When the smoke cleared, the amount of memos, bulletins, notices, for-your-information copies, and the like were reduced 38 percent. The paper, printing, and circulation labor costs and, above all, the time people saved were unbelievable.

The value of having time saved by the receivers is one that is usually overlooked. If you have twenty-six people receiving a memo, and reading and digesting time amounts to four minutes, there goes one hour and forty-four minutes. If that is multiplied by ten items a day, five days a week, it works out to 4,006 hours per year... and we only started with one little old memo that involved only four teeney weeney minutes.

As far as the cost-benefit relationship of communications, how do you decide whether to initiate a new bulletin or, better yet, is there an ongoing program to evaluate periodically the discontinuance of these things? Many times, reports can be eliminated. Perhaps their once-important purpose is no longer a factor. Usually, you will find several reports that can be pared down and combined. Many times there will be an overlap of reports or information. The communication of information goes far beyond a letter or a news bulletin. Look carefully and check your benefits.

Look at the value to franchisees of the content in your monthly house organ. What are the frequency and content of regional and national meetings? How is the training program evaluated? How and when are your training, operations, advertising, and other manuals updated? Do you have a service award program? Does the president communicate directly with field offices? Is it necessary for him to do so? Are your regional inspectors or representatives your prime communications link with your franchisee operations? Is there a planned owner/franchisee headquarters visitation or tour? The key word is *planned*. What do you want to communicate? Is there a communications benefit from other staff contacts with the franchisees? The list goes on and on, but keep that number-one objective in mind. What is the desired goal? *R*...Reaction.

Are your communications getting through to the right people? Has anyone checked the mailing list lately? If you send all information to the franchisee at the store or outlet, what about his two investor partners, who rarely come to the store? Public relations with them is important, isn't it? Lack of knowledge about a problem could be vital. If trouble develops between franchisor and franchisee, those other two parties will have a lot to say. They must be kept informed about how valuable the franchisor has been to the outlet they have invested in.

Getting through is always a problem. Sometimes it takes a constant bombardment of information for people to recognize your value as their franchisor. Your situation and techniques must be continually reevaluated.

I told you earlier to conserve and cut back, now I am saying to send out information by the pound. What you do hinges on value received. Each situation must be measured. In some cases it is necessary constantly to show the franchisee how to turn on the faucet. About the sixth bulletin that says, "The cold is on the right and the hot is on the left" will get through to him. If that kind of repetition is needed, then you must do it. Just use different words each time, even though all six wind up with the same conclusion.

THE IMPORTANCE OF FEEDBACK

As I mentioned earlier, you must make it attractive and easy for franchisees and/or their managers to communicate back with you. This feedback of ideas as well as the "being heard" psychology are vital to every organization. Recognition is probably the cornerstone of success for getting feedback. Anything worthwhile should receive acknowledgment from your offices and then in your house organ. You might wish to place some dollar value on different classifications of ideas. Then, if the feedback provides an idea of benefit to the system, you can make an award which will carry public relations value to the property as well.

One company I know has certain people in the operations department who call the franchisees once a week. This technique often wards off problems or bad feelings before they reach the point where the franchisee is disturbed and calls you. There is a caution with this or any contact with the franchise owner: Be absolutely sure you or someone else gets back in touch and lets him know what has happened to his request, suggestion, or comment. Never leave him wondering, which would lead him to believe that you are not interested in what he thinks.

It is important not to represent your company as the great white father who knows all the answers and does nothing but give advice. This can only be interpreted by franchisees (or anyone) as a parent-child relationship. Rebellion will come along sometime, even if it is later when the child grows up. Others and their ideas are important and valuable. Work very hard on allowing the communications channel to flow back to you.

24

The Architecture and Design Department

Dos and Don'ts in Setting It Up

I have always admired the immortals whose creations have brought happiness to millions of people ... Frank Lloyd Wright, Ludwig von Beethoven, Vincent van Gogh, Charles Dickens, and, of course, Jack Daniels.

Architectural creations are very nice. Be sure yours are functional and cost-conscious as well. Often the creative genius of architects can obscure functionality and can skyrocket costs to where the franchisees' profit-and-loss bottom line is not as attractive as that of your competitors. If your system requires construction of a building and/or extensive interior design, you need to be on top of this.

Many times I have had architects and experienced contractors say we cannot build our buildings for the figures I have quoted. This is after glancing at an existing building and applying what they think is a general square-foot cost. Of course, this is based on their prior experience. They will say the same thing after a quick glance at the plans. All the while, I know what I'm quoting them because of final bids on current construction of the same building. This is because our designers are thoroughly in tune with appearances and costs. It is a matter of assessing your desires intelligently and then conforming.

HOW TO KNOW WHAT TO BELIEVE

Often franchisors allow architects to draw up something that appeals to their eye. But don't forget the psychological motivations of your potential customers. I worked with a franchisor who was cognizant of these factors. Because of the particular factors he found would attract his customers, he made a conscious decision to have his buildings designed in a less aesthetically appealing way than they could have been for the same money. Several years later he decided that his system had public awareness, so he decided to do away with the garish exterior and make the exterior colors more aesthetically appealing. He hired a designer to pick the new monochromatic colors, and they repainted one of their buildings. Business suffered in that location. His product was low priced, and that is what the exterior appearance had originally conveyed. His building now looked too good to evoke the economical image.

As a young man, I spent five years with the world's largest advertising agency. The education was fantastic. When you stand in a supermarket with a clipboard for hours asking customers why they picked the red-and-yellow box rather than the blue-and-green one, you learn a lot. There is a psychology that goes into every facet of your operation. Make decisions carefully. They may seem small and even unimportant, but those little things, when combined with one hundred other little things, may make the difference in whether you get to add three more zeros to the bottom line of your profit-and-loss statement. By the way, the franchisor who painted his building the pretty, monochromatic colors...he changed it back to the original garish colors. His business went back up.

CHANGE MAY OR MAY NOT BE GOOD

Another consideration is design flexibility. How much will you allow? Potential franchisees also have definite ideas, and some will push very hard for what they think is best. Consider carefully: Is there real prostitution to your system if some deviation is allowed, or is it of little consequence? Be cautious not to let "pride of authorship" cloud your thinking. What sales value could this decision have? You must be realistically tuned to all the psychological factors as well as to the obvious realities of normal business practices.

Should you ever have an in-house or out-of-house architectural department? Without knowing any details of your product, desires, money availability, and so on, I cannot answer that. Once more, watch that ego. Some companies that have architectural departments could probably cut their costs in half if they cut down to a small one- or two-person department and contracted out the rest. They do not do so because of some feeling the boss has about "his" people doing it all. His chest gets bigger when he is showing a guest around, or perhaps he just does not want to think about change. The habit of not questioning whether a thing is wrong often gives it the superficial appearance of being right.

25

The Franchise
Sales Department

Here Is What You Need to Sell Franchises

*My boss told me to go out this week
and sell two franchises ... What
is a franchise?*

That opening quote could have happened a few years ago, but I hope it would not be possible today. With all the legislation on the books, you had better have your salespeople well tuned to all the legal dos and don'ts. The Bible tells us that Samson slew thousands with the jawbone of an ass. Many companies have gotten into trouble with the same weapon. Good companies have had to lay out bundles of cash over something said by an uninformed salesperson. The sales department must be trained in legal aspects as well as product knowledge and salesmanship.

After all is said and done, there is a lot more said than done. Promises or statements innocently made can be devastating. They may not even be comments that could get you into legal trouble; they may be the kind that changes the franchisee's attitude toward you. It is all in how they see it. At times, it might be the way the salesperson paraphrases the statement.

I remember when our boys were three and six years old. They had one of those little pet turtles that you keep in a fishbowl with a few rocks and a little water. One day they found the turtle on its back, not moving. They laid him on the table and for the next hour there was still no movement. As I walked in, they rushed up with tears in their eyes to tell me their turtle was dead. I checked the turtle and he seemed lifeless. In an effort to calm the boys, I suggested he have a turtle funeral. I told them they should call four or five of their friends, we could get some ice cream and cookies, play a few games, then bury the turtle in the flower bed in the backyard. They thought that was great, called their friends, and I started getting out the ice cream and cookies. About that time, my oldest son saw the turtle move. He shouted with delight, "He isn't dead! We don't have to have a turtle funeral!" One of the other boys said, "Nuts—no party. . . . Let's kill him so we can have the ice cream and cookies." It is all in what one expects.

To have franchisees expecting more than what comes about is bad. To have them expecting less and have things turn out better is great. You wind up with pleased franchisees. They buy additional franchises, recommend you to their friends and relatives, praise you to other potential franchisees who may call them before they sign up.

SUCCESSFUL SALES TOOLS USED BY OTHERS

There is no need for me to attempt to write about any of the various techniques of salesmanship. Thousands of books are already out on that subject. In connection with franchising, there is one tool that has been used very successfully by many. That is the video cassette or film strip with taped audio. It not only does a sales job, but it offers great legal protection. It saved my company a bundle once.

It was in my younger days as a salesman. Since I had advertising agency experience, I decided to do my own film strip. First, I wrote out the basic sales presentation. I made sure the legal disclosures were woven throughout the entire program. Next, I took 35-mm slide photographs of all the various things that would tie in with the script. I did a matching cassette tape of the script, then had the slides mounted into a filmstrip. There was our first film presentation. (Of course, today the company has a professional announcer with the proper tempo of music in the background and all the fanfare and psychology that goes with it. But it still has those legal points woven throughout.)

About five years after every salesperson began using the film presentation, we had a disgruntled franchisee who decided he could do better as an independent. He looked for a way to get out of the franchise and finally sued us for misrepresentations. He claimed that various things were supposedly said and not said when we sold him the franchise. Just prior to going to court, we set up a final meeting with the franchisee, his attorney, and ours. At that meeting, we pulled out that old film presentation we had shown him originally. He had already admitted seeing the film initially. After his attorney saw it, we never went to court. However, we did settle with them so they could get out of the system. We felt it would be better if they were gone.

I might add that after getting out, their sales went down and they finally put the motel up for sale. In selling it, they misrepresented the figures to the buyer. Later, the buyer sued for misrepresentation and to have the sale set aside. The judge found the seller guilty and ordered to motel taken back.

There are other things a film does. It makes sure everyone is singing the same song. You are sure the best-thought-out sales presentation is the one the potential franchisee is hearing. It gets in all the important points. It usually has the potential franchisee's undivided attention. It tells the story faster than any salesperson possibly could. It makes your company seem more professional.

There are several inexpensive filmstrip or cassette and tape presentation units that are smaller than a normal briefcase. I have found the size and weight to be a big factor in getting the salesperson to use the units every time. They don't mind using them in the office, but when it comes to carrying these units on the road, they avoid using them if they are bulky.

I cannot overemphasize the importance of the legal position a salesperson can place you in. In October 1979, a regulation went into effect that is referred to as the FTC Rule. The common law practice is that when an agreement is reduced to writing and the contents therein say the document supercedes any oral statements, that is valid. Under the FTC Rule, when your sales representative states something to a potential franchisee and he relies on it in making his decision to buy, that statement survivies the written agreement. If he sues later, how can you prove your representative did not say the things the franchisee, his wife, and her mother swear he did? It becomes a very real problem. Therefore, training, integrity, and the capability of being totally straight are very important. Things like printed brochures and flyers become valuable. It is a good idea to have the franchisee sign that he has received and read that information. You have to get his signature on the FTC disclosure documents; why not cover the other bases? It may be a great assistance if trouble arises.

One of your best sales tools can be your satisfied franchisees. If cultivated properly, they can furnish you leads that are somewhat qualified. Part of the cultivation might be merely letting them know you are interested in putting another outlet on the other side of town. This will stir their thinking and perhaps they will decide to expand. If not, they may help locate a friend or relative who is interested in getting into the business. You can depend on the fact that a potential franchisee will certainly call an established franchisee to see what he thinks of you and your business opportunity. This alone is definitely worth your cultivating efforts.

SHOULD YOU LET SOMEONE ELSE SELL YOUR FRANCHISE?

The question always comes up eventually about letting someone else sell your franchise. If you seriously consider this, it will probably be through some franchise development sales and/or consulting company. There are some considerations you should weigh carefully.

I have just outlined the seriousness of controlling what your salespeople say. If an outside firm is working for you, it is much harder to oversee. You lose a large degree of control. Often these firms employ high-pressure guns to sell. The firm and the salesperson are probably on commission, so they push hard. Now there is nothing really wrong with pushing to do a job, but the control is tough. I once heard a story about a franchisor who hired an outside firm because "Their salespeople can say things my employees aren't supposed to say." That franchisor has either not sought legal advice or has received some that is bad. The law just doesn't work that way. You say, "Well, I could contract to protect myself with the sales company." You can put it in writing and have 16 notaries witness it, but those sales representatives are your agents. The key word is *your.* In addition, if you wind up with several suits against you from franchisees, who do you think will have to be defended? Right! If those suits take your company down the tube, what then?

The topic of outside sales firms has been discussed in workshop sessions held by the IFA on numerous occasions. Among those who have tried it and those who have not, the basic conclusions have been against hiring outside assistance.

Now let me defend the sales firms. I'm sure many of them do a creditable job. Your checking should be extensive and your decision perhaps tempered by a second opinion from someone not in the business. I believe it would be tough for someone in the sales business to come in and do a feasibility study on your concept and divorce themselves enough to be totally objective. After all, if they come up negative in evaluating your possibilities for success, they don't get a job.

Some will do a sales effort with you covering the costs and paying them a commission. Since you are paying the costs, they can't lose, even if the proposition is not successful. Some will also reduce their commission and take a piece of the action in your company. They can't lose again. You pay the costs. If it is a failure, you are out. If it is a success, they get a piece of your company without having to buy it or risk anything. It is a sort of "heads they win, tails you lose" situation. Thus, be wary of the sales firm evaluating your potential. Objectivity is difficult when dealing with one's self. Be careful also of your own evaluation. Your heart and your pocketbook are involved. Those two often interfere with sound business realism. I know a real estate broker who has been in the business for twenty years. He had a large home in a nice section of town. When his children grew up and left home, he decided to sell it and move to a smaller place. Wisely, he paid another broker to appraise his house for him. He said he knew his personal knowledge of all the work he had put into the house over the years and his love for the home would interfere with logical, sound judgment as a broker and appraiser. He was a wise man.

WHAT ABOUT SALES TERRITORIES?

Now let's take a look at territory. There are two types. One is the salesperson's territory; the other is the franchisee's territory. Let's take the salesperson first.

Your stage of growth will possibly determine what you want to do. Just don't give away the farm in your enthusiasm. I know, the whole country (world) is open to you, but as you spread you will have to adjust. If your salespeople truly understand this (put it in writing for them), it will not be so tough to split up the area. Another factor is the nature of the salesman. He is charged up to sell. He will be willing to go anywhere to make a deal. You may find he is spreading himself so thin with travel time that he is cutting into his potential by 25 percent or 50 percent. In addition, if you are paying his expenses—and you are, either through his commissions or directly—it is costing you much more than it should.

The other problem for you is servicing. If your sales are jumping from state to state, it is expensive for your operations, inspections, and training personnel to service the franchise properly. If your long-range plan and your bankroll can handle it, then okay. Just plan your strategy and go.

How about the territory for the franchisee? How much protection do you give him? This is a problem that requires consultation. To solve it, one party needs a franchise attorney, the other a franchise consultant. The

Sherman Antitrust Act became involved with this area many years ago. Since then, the courts have gradually moved in the direction that says perhaps territories do not cut down on competition. I believe that in some situations it could even help competition. Here we start with what the law calls "rules of reason." Those are legal words of art that are like painting a picture of a landscape: If you have four different artists, you will get four different pictures. The franchise attorney and the business consultant will have to work closely with you on this. You are planning a serious part of your contract. It runs for years into the future and it must be as nearly right as possible when you begin.

There are many franchisors who did not have the franchising consultant to start with and who have either been cut off in certain markets or have spent a fortune to buy back those areas. Be sure psychologically and from a future business standpoint that you have designed well.

A question: Is is absolutely necessary to grant a territory at all? I have advised serveral firms how to structure their sales presentation and their franchise agreement so it is not necessary. Here a lot more information is needed about your product/service and long-range expansion goals. The variables are so numerous it would be impossible to generalize here.

TOO MANY SALES CAN PUT YOU OUT OF BUSINESS

Let's say you have built a sales organization. It is fired up and selling. Would you think I was crazy if I suggested you might need to pull it in and slow down? Let me relate a real-life story that took place about nine years ago.

There was a franchisee who had been very successful. He had outlets in seven or eight states and he was making millions of dollars. He had a home-office operation that was larger than many franchisors. He had been in the business for years and thought he knew the franchise business from the franchisor's side too. After all, it wasn't that complicated, and he had worked closely with his franchisor for many years. He knew of a sizable hamburger chain that had all company stores. It was regional and not too spread out geographically. The chain was having financial problems. He bought control of the small chain and closed all the stores. With his marketing department and advertising agency, he began choosing a new name, color scheme, menu, and so on. The decision was to create an entirely new image for his hamburger chain. He was going to become a franchisor.

Finally, the grand opening day came. All outlets opened at the same time. Since they were all in the same region, the marketing was tremendous. They hit the radio, TV, and newspaper; they did direct mail with coupons and various daily specials. This continued for about sixty days. Almost everyone had heard their name by now. Business was great. People were standing in lines from four to ten deep at registers. This was the beginning of their downfall.

Their sales efforts were paying off very well, but their people had not been thoroughly trained. There were not enough employees to service the crowd of customers. Not being thoroughly trained, the service was less than the public demanded. Likewise, the food was not up to par because of the large quantities that the huge number of customers were buying. The customers came once, but they did not come back the second time. In about a year the chain was out of business because of too much business on the front end which could not be properly serviced.

I have seen the same thing happen to other franchisors. If the hamburger chain had the correct controls and trained people in place before they attempted to blast off, they might be alive today. They thought they did. They thought they knew. They did not think being a franchisor was that hard. It is.

Have your shake-down cruise and all necessary areas functioning before you start off at full speed. I am not saying this applies uniformly to all types of franchisors, but it does apply to most. Measure yourself wisely and plan accordingly.

What and how should you pay your salespeople? This has been the subject of several workshop sessions among franchisors. Some use straight salary, some use salary plus expenses, others pay salary plus commission, some pay straight commission. From there you can dream up an arrangement, and it's probably being used. Your system possibly dictates a portion of the plan you should use. I cannot lay out your plan in this book since I do not know your business.

THIRTEEN ITEMS A SALESPERSON NEEDS IN ORDER TO SELL

What does a salesperson need? Generally, it will be some or all of the following:

1. Application form
2. Question-and-answer form

3. Franchise/license agreement
4. Advertising brochures
5. Brochures of services you offer
6. List of references and endorsements
7. Training brochure
8. Film presentation
9. Presentation book
10. Company financial information
11. Disclosure packets
12. Site selection criteria
13. Advertising assistance information

TWENTY-THREE THINGS A POTENTIAL FRANCHISEE WANTS TO KNOW

When designing your information, it would be wise to place yourself in the position of the potential franchisee. Questions they probably think about are:

1. Is this franchisor selective in those he accepts into the system?
2. Does he check experience, character, financial stability, and reputation?
3. Is the company forward-looking and aggressive?
4. Does the advertising seem up with the times?
5. Can I advertise locally?
6. Are there quantity buying advantages?
7. Does the contract seem fair to both parties?
8. Will the company provide continuing assistance?
9. Under what conditions could I lose the franchise?
10. Can I renew the franchise upon its termination?
11. Can the franchise be transferred?
12. Are manuals and sales aids available?
13. How are the advertising funds administered?
14. If there is a product, is it packaged properly?
15. Are all understandings in the franchise agreement?
16. What fees are charged?
17. Are the prices generally competitive?

18. If there is a territory, is it adequate?
19. What services do the fees include?
20. Can I engage in other businesses?
21. Will I be proud to be associated with this company and its products/ services?
22. Do the references offered check out well?
23. Can the territory be changed on me?

WHY YOU SHOULD GET ALL THE BUYERS TOGETHER

One day I walked into the local paint store and there in front of me was a sign: "Husbands wanting to purchase specially mixed colors must have signed notes from their wives." In almost any franchise opportunity, this same philosophy applies. Get all the parties together for your presentation. If your opportunity is one that will most likely involve the husband and wife in some way, then be sure they both are in on all the conversations. If yours is an investor-type opportunity that will most likely involve a larger sum of money, it is just as important to get all the potential partners together. There are several reasons for getting everyone in on the act even though they may only want to be passive in their participation. The main reason is that they will probably not be passive later in their vocal or actual dissenting attitudes. Many want to be silent partners or silent investors. Quite often they do not want to attend your presentations. You may not be able to get them but, if at all possible, try to reach them. The uninformed, unaware, and silent participant is often the one who gripes and encorages the active partner to "protest too much." There may be later confrontations with some franchisees. The informed partners are less likely to be the problem children. This matter of information is especially serious in the initial stages of your sale. The one who does not attend your meeting may be the one who says no when the attendee tries to relay your information as best he can. Your sale may never be made.

WHERE TO GET SALES LEADS

An additional area we need to cover is the sales lead. Where does it first come from?

1. Newspaper ads
2. Radio or TV ads
3. Trade shows
4. Existing franchisees
5. Direct mail
6. Special seminars
7. Industry publication
8. Leads from:
   - Suppliers
   - Friends
   - Employees
   - Competitors who already have an operation nearby
   - Business associates
9. PR from planned in-house sources

Any or all of these can be expensive. I presume you have budget restraints, which will provide some guidelines. Number 9 is an item that may cost very little if you have a planned approach.

HOW TO GET FREE ADVERTISING AND FREE LEADS

When we started our company, we had to go the public relations (free advertising for creation of public awareness) route because we did not have any money. During the first two and a half years, our paid advertising expenditure was less than twenty-five dollars. Yet we sold over one hundred franchises. I planned the PR route and went to work on it. There is a method or way of thinking when one goes to look for a newsworthy item that can give you public acceptance and awareness and convey to the public a desire to buy what you have. Naturally, if the media smells unpaid advertising in the story, they will never print it. This method of thought/ story/creativity can be learned fairly easily by whoever is handling this area for you.

There is a factor in connection with this creativity that shocks me constantly, and that is the number of marketing directors who have not already learned how to think this way. They are trained by schools, agencies, or bosses who do not know and the ignorance perpetuates itself. Even large companies with sizably professional staffs more than likely do not have the necessary knowledge. I assisted in laying out a simplified program toward this end for the IFA. The idea was to create awareness, among the public and perhaps franchisors, of what the franchising method of marketing means to individuals as well as to our country and world. With very little expense, the word was placed before 19 million people within the first six months.

I say learning it is simple. It is, yet I would have to know your specific business first in order to teach you how to think of/create a story. After the story is created, with proper public interest invested, one takes the proper photographs (emphasis is on the word *proper*), writes the story in final form, and delivers it to the media. You have done their work for them. They need a hot story before the deadline, so they mark up yours and run it.

Again, I cannot overemphasize the importance of using the creative process for the story and photo. At first it is not an easy thing to think up, but it is an easy thing to learn to do acccurately. I would estimate that the advertising value of published stories our company received during those first two and a half years probably exceeded $525,000. That may not seem a large number to you, but for us at that time—and for a paid cost of less than twenty-five dollars—it is a colossal number. By the way, we have recently engineered another coup: The leading industry magazine gave us the cover and an eleven-page story.

What medium should you use to generate sales leads? Again, I would have to know what business you are in. Some publications perform better on certain days for certain types of business. Your results may be satisfactory, but nowhere near what they could be for the same money if you know what medium, what day, what type of ad. Advertising is nebulous in many cases. This is why it is so important to know. To be able to go to school accurately on the knowledge others have acquired can save you thousands of dollars—and possibly even your whole company.

One good source for leads is often the existing franchisee owner. Do you have an incentive program for him? You must be careful here. There are possible legal entanglements. Yet it is a good source: cultivate it well.

Some place inquiry cards on the counter or in the office of every operation. You will acquire a lot of information from the number of people who jot down their name and address and deposit same in a mailbox.

So your sales department will know how to proceed, you must outline all the possibilities you will consider. For instance, are you interested in joint ventures with potential franchisess? When a franchise is sold but the buyer is short on net worth or cash to start, will you come in for a partnership? This and numerous other possibilities should be decided and fully discussed with the sales department. When they are in the field they do not have time to wait for you and your board to hold the next meeting. They need to know so they can react to either close or kill a potential deal.

How do you feel about an existing employee becoming a franchisee? I know one system that encourages this. They have built a large company. In later years, the real growth has come from company employees, existing franchisees, and their friends, What a way to go! Everybody is presold!

Do you, can you, will you get involved in the real estate? This can be a large, profitable area, depending on your type of franchise and your financial capabilities. Again, this is an area of delicate legal and management programming.

Remember that saying, "Nothing happens until a sale is made"? Do you believe it? You will probably say yes. Remember also: "Actions speak louder than words." If you believe it, what type of support are you giving your sales department and their marketing efforts? Are they your better-paid people? Do you hold them in high esteem and boost their egos in front of others? Do you let the other departments know how important it is for everyone to sell and support the sales department? Nothing happens until a sale is made.

26

The Site Approval Committee

How to Get the Right Location

*If you knew what I know, you would
not disagree with me.*

Okay, so tell me what you know. Then I will know and we will see if I agree
with you. Without knowing what business you are in, I cannot tell you
specifically how to pick a site for your company. The criteria for a fast-food
company would certainly not be the same as they are for a mini-
warehouse. The important thing is to expose the committee to all the
knowledge the members truly need. Then they can make intelligent
decisions.

   I believe committees should be made up of three people: one who is
always out of the country, one who is sick at home, and the chairman, who
makes a decision and moves things forward quickly. A story is told of the
former president of General Motors, Mr. Charles Kettering. When the
radio broke the news of Lindbergh crossing the Atlantic, someone rushed
into Mr. Kettering's office and said, "Charlie Lindbergh just flew the
Atlantic alone." He looked up and said, "Heck, that's nothing, let him try it
with a committee." If you have an accurate mathematical/analytical success
model, one person can weigh the facts. If you do not, I suggest you have a
committee of persons who are very knowledgeable. You or your franchisee
cannot afford to have a failure.

   Today the process of site selection is usually more scientific, but I
remember many who would have taken the dart and thrown it at a map.
This was the formal approval process. If the dart stuck within nine
thousand miles of the location, it was approved. That is perhaps a little
overstated, but many have used what they refer to as a "gut feeling." If the

person doing the deciding has been in the business for a while, perhaps this reaction is valid. I think what he would be saying is, "I have weighed what I have seen and read against my years of successes and failures. I have mentally computed the reasons for success or failure against various locations and my decision on this location is..." This has a lot of validity. It is the brain computer compared to the mechanical computer. The brain is sometimes wrong, but probably more often is right.

One thing is for sure: Without one or more of your people viewing the location, it generally is hard to make a realistic and honest evaluation of the property. In almost every type of franchise, local information must be generated by someone who understands your system or at least the industry in which you are involved.

There are firms which develop models for their computers to play with. When enough of the right ingredients for a successful location can be fed into this mechanical brain, it can come pretty close to calculating your chances for success. If you are small or just starting out, you may have to wait a while before the model operation can be programmed for your organization, unless your operations are closely akin to competitors. If that is the case, there may already be existing information.

WHAT YOU NEED TO KNOW ABOUT A LOCATION

What type of information is needed? Again, it depends on your type of franchise. Generally, it might be:

1. Traffic and street information with relation to:
   - stoplights
   - one- or two-way streets
   - number of traffic lanes
   - turn lanes
   - medians or dividers
   - number of cars
   - number of walking traffic and their demographics
   - income of traffic
   - speed permitted
   - street changes pending
   - area housing demographics
   - employment type

- destination of traffic
- origination of traffic
- commercial traffic counts
- sex of traffic
- age of traffic
- directional visibility

2. Utilities and their capacities available to site:
   - water
   - sewage
   - electricity
   - telephone
   - gas
   - alternatives if any one of the above is not available

3. Population density in a given radius
   - complete demographics on population

4. Business demographics in the area considered

5. Churches, schools, medical facilities, recreation center, etc.

6. Breakdown of competition by classifications

7. Desire/need of the potential buyers

8. Voids that may exist in the market area

9. Your potential for filling those voids as well as capturing business from competition

10. Possibility of creating a desire/need among potential customers

11. Possibility of market changes in the future.

The list can go on and on. Some answers will come from the compilation of earlier statistics. You may not need nearly all the information listed. Success and time will improve your screening ability. It is certainly comforting to be able to detail a mathematical model location selection process. The process may be one that utilizes multiple regression equations in order to forecast probable sales and net profit or loss for the first through the third or fourth years of operation.

COMPUTER MODELS FOR SELECTING LOCATIONS

I am familiar with a mechanical process that is used exclusively by one franchisor. If the computer says no, he will reject the site. They have over

5,000 locations. The president of the company tells me the model has not been more than 5 percent off in predicting the gross sales for a potential operation in several years. Wouldn't that type of assurance be comforting to you and your pocketbook?

If you come up with a success every time, do you know what will happen? Right! Your franchisees and their friends will want to open more and more locations. First thing you know, you will be getting to where only your franchisees get first crack at any potential site. Then if you are not careful, the whole country is sold out. Guess what? That is exactly what happened to this friend of mine and his company. Success breeds success. If franchisees are successful, so are you.

Unless your business is almost exactly like a competitor's, you will have to wait until you get a number of locations before you can build a model. Even if you are like a competitor, it is unlikely you can get the technical information on his locations to build your model. Even with a number of outlets, you still need personal judgment. I suggest that judgment be high-caliber. That is, be well versed on your business, with a lot of common sense.

Whether you have a mechanical model or a committee, the relationships of the survey information should be set up so the information occupies relative importance in reference to its effect on total sales. This is difficult. It takes experience and a set of some successful operations to mock up the evaluation process. Some items will seem insignificant; by themselves they probably are, however, they may be very important if you have twenty of these items and they average a worth to sales volume of ½ to 1 percent each. You quickly can see that can amount to 10 percent of total sales. It may mean the difference between success and failure.

The process can be expensive. Perhaps in early years a physical mechanical approach must be taken for various reasons, including cost. When you can afford it and you have the availability of successful operations, do not let further time pass without a system that is scientifically objective. It is too important to your business. Failure is very, very expensive. Success is inexpensive. In addition, the process itself saves you money. For example, the establishing of relationships to find coefficients is difficult and temperamental. The cost to put them together runs high, but on a computer it can be cheap in the long run. Once developed, one can pull off twenty-five to thirty-five coefficients in five or ten minutes. By hand, it would take thirty-five clerks six to eight months to do the same thing with their little calculators. Once these are developed, you now have objectivity. The human is capable of performing with intuition and reasonable accuracy. That may be the security factor for further success assurance.

When you start building your model, I personally think it is okay to build in allowable error—how much error depends on your type of business. Let's say a 6 percent error, plus or minus, is allowable. With that we can assume a probability of 94 percent accuracy. Allowing for the error factor cuts down greatly on the cost of the model work, and 94 percent is possibly enough accuracy for total assurance of the site in question. The 94 percent factor also recognizes the possibility that on rare occasions there may be factors that are so unusual they could upset the entire program of the model.

Since we have been discussing models, I might add a point about beefing up sales at a later date. There are things you will purposely or accidentally be doing in locations which produce varying degrees of profit or loss. These things will be out of the norm in day-to-day operation of a "standard" location. The programming of a model can lead to new and greater sales heights. Many managers will give hip-pocket versions of why something does or does not work. Some of this analysis is valid, some is not.

There may be cases where three combinations produce one type of sales results while two combinations fail. These facts, together with other scientifically designed questions, can enable you to tell your locations how much increase to expect for how much cost, as well as the alternates, which may be used as backups. With all this varying information, the franchisee can then accurately choose the actions which promise the greatest results to fit his area and desires.

Market feasibility studies are generally good. I say generally because it depends on the qualifications of the firm or individuals making the survey and the depth they go into. In any event, the computer model, if properly fed the correct information, is more accurate in my opinion. That is because the model is based on the actual experiences of operating successes and failures. The feasibility study is largely based on the conjecture of potential customers and what they will do. I realize there is overlap in both areas. Both are good, but one seems to be better. When you begin to take advantage of mechanical brains for your business, you will be surprised. The pleasant results will show in additional knowledge, ability, and success.

WHEN TO USE REAL ESTATE BROKERS

Should your site committee (or sales department) utilize real estate brokers? If you are large and have an operating real estate department, your answer may be "Yes" or "No." Let me presume you are not large and do not have a full-blown real estate division.

For most companies, I believe a combination method of in-house and out-of-house services might serve best. Professional brokers get paid a commission like all other brokers. You think you can save some money by bypassing the broker? Not so, in my opinion. I have been a broker for twenty years plus, and I still have an active real estate business. Although in recent years I do not personally participate in it a great deal, I do own it and sit in on general overall policy decisions.

I am firmly convinced that a good broker is worth every penny to the buyer, the seller, the franchisor, and the franchisee. Let me tell you how strongly I believe this. I put my money where my mouth is. Over the years, I have been in on the negotiations of many deals. I concluded a long time ago that the buyer and the seller or the lessor and the lessee were at opposite ends of any negotiation or deal. One wants all he can get in every aspect of the deal; the other's point is just the opposite. People who are totally opposed in goals are not best suited to negotiate with each other. In steps the broker. His goal is solely to put the deal together for both parties. If both do not agree, there is no deal. He works for both parties. I know he usually represents the seller from a legal standpoint, but isn't the seller's goal also to put the deal together? Actually, the ultimate goal of all parties is the same. This is the broker's role. I am firmly convinced that brokers usually earn what I pay them. Right—I said pay them. Even though I am a broker, I use other brokers for myself.

Note one thing I said earlier. I used the word *good* when speaking of a broker. The important factor is not nececessarily the real estate firm, it is the individual you deal with. Granted, some firms have exclusive advantages in cutting a deal the way you want it, but it is usually the ability of the individual negotiating for you that makes the difference.

Now back to my use of brokers. They get better deals than I could by negotiating directly with the opposite party. I have just closed a deal on some commercial property in which I paid the agent a full 10 percent commission. I did not co-broker it through my company or cut his commission one dime. Why? Because he got the deal. The land was the keystone piece I owned in the center of property near a huge shopping mall, the last undeveloped land in the area. A big New York public company wanted it all. They had to deal with me: There was no other land available, and I had the center lot. Yet I called the agent in on it. Crazy? No, because he successfully negotiated the price I quoted him. It was high; it was more than the property was worth; it was unrealistic; it was what I thought was near that psychological point of queering the deal completely. When you get close to that point, you had better get someone in to handle it. The broker pulled the deal together.

How about buying? Same thing. About a year ago, I called a sharp broker and told him what I was looking for in a commercial structure. Four months later, he called me and said he had it. The price, terms, and so on were not as I liked. We put our heads together and, sixty days later, he had negotiated "my" deal. Sure, the seller paid his commission, but I paid it indirectly as the buyer. No one sells, no one buys, no one gets a commission unless all agree. I am convinced that this broker's professionalism and objectivity were responsible for this deal. I probably could not have gotten it if I had been head to head with the seller.

By the way, after buying the property, I renovated it, built the business up, and listed it with the same broker for sale. A few weeks later he brought me a signed contract on which I will make almost $600,000 after his commission is paid.

Twenty-seven years ago, I decided not to handle my own deals, but to use someone else. I have continued that policy since and have only pleasant thoughts of dollar signs to sleep on.

HOW TO PICK A GOOD BROKER OR SALESPERSON

Now, about picking a good broker or salesperson. Make sure his financial knowledge is what you want. So many just do not have it. In addition, it is essential that he be good at creative thinking and talking. If he has only worked on three or four deals like you are contemplating, or if he has only been in the business a short time, beware. He probably just does not have the background and life experience you need. He must be creative. Standard deals can be cut out with a cookie cutter, but that doesn't necessarily make a good transaction. When you or the seller hit an impasse, you need the broker's creativity to put together a passable deal. He becomes extremely valuable then. His abilities will show up when he is on his feet in front of the other party. Pick the right individual.

Be sure he understands your desires, otherwise he will waste a lot of time running around the country. This is also why it is important to have someone with common sense. If he doesn't have that he will attempt to show you everything on the market in hopes that something might click. This is a waste of your time and poor salesmanship on his part. You have the wrong man.

Another plus for real estate agents! If you were going to hire staff people with the ability and experience discussed, they would currently cost you $70,000 to $125,000 a year each. That cuts into your budget pretty heavily. Then, too, if you are a rapidly expanding company, you may want locations in twenty different states at once. The travel and lodging expenses alone could be very high. There is an advantage to having twenty different people out there looking on your behalf...none of whom are on your payroll or expense account.

You do need someone on your staff to coordinate with these brokers. It would be ideal if you had a broker on staff who understands all of these intricacies. If not, certainly get someone who has real estate experience of some type. You are dealing with big bucks, and knowledge paid for is usually well worthwhile.

How do you go about selecting a real estate broker? You might contact the local bank and savings-and-loan mortgage closing officers. Carefully describe the qualifications and the personality type you are looking for. The Society of Industrial Realtors roster might also be a place to look.

After narrowing it down, go see each broker. Do not give away information about what your qualifications or desires in a real estate agent are. Quiz her first so you can tell a bit about the individual. Question her financial abilities, personality, creativity, and desire to work. After all, some brokers are so busy you may get a halfhearted effort; some are financially fat and possibly at an age where they want to play golf all day.

Has she worked for franchisors before? What areas of the business does she specialize in? If you want, does she have investors to build and lease to you? Does she have builders available to her? What loan connections can she assist with? What are her site data abilities? Does she maintain census tracts and other information in her office? Does she have planning department connections in the city if help in zoning and such is necessary? All of this type of information and more will help you decide whether to choose or eliminate a broker.

Should you work with her on an exclusive basis? It depends. Often in selling you will only get your best marketing and sales effort if you list exclusively. However, in some towns it is not a practice to list commercial property exclusively. But remember I said "best marketing and sales effort." A broker will spend more money on promoting your sale if they are protected. It is an economic fact of business.

On buying or leasing, if you attempt to work with several brokers, the good ones will usually drop you. That too is an economic fact of business.

She still occasionally will send some information on a piece of property she listed exclusively. But she will not keep you on top of her list.

You may pick a weak sister sometimes, but when you hit a good, loyal one, hold on to her. Do business with her; refer customers to her. Prove you are protecting her even if you do not have an exclusive agreement. She will treat you likewise and the relationship will be worthwhile. Remember, real estate and the improvements thereon are often the largest single dollar items you may be involved in. Be good and straight with the person who is buying or selling for you.

27

The Training Department

Why and How You Should Invest Heavily in Training

The Chinese word for crisis *is written by combining the symbols for the words* danger *and* opportunity.

Many an optimist has become rich by simply buying out a pessimist. What is the difference? Attitude! I know two partners who started their franchising company the same time we started our company. After about three years, one became cynical about the business; he saw only crisis after crisis. The other saw opportunity. Finally, the partner who saw opportunity offered to buy out the other. He took the deal. The remaining partner had high hopes and believed everyone. In three more years, with a success on his hands, he took his company public, kept about one-half the stock for himself and still put around $5 million in his pocket after taxes. In two more years, he merged with a large corporation, put $48 million more in his pocket and stayed on as head of his company under a very nice contract. Can you imagine what the pessimist partner who sold for a paltry sum is saying? It is all in attitude—how we see things.

I could fill up the rest of the book with stories like this, but you know many of them already, I am sure. Now what does this have to do with your training department?

WHY YOU SHOULD FIRST DECIDE TO BE A "Y" COMPANY

The training department is conveying your attitudes to the new people who will go into the field and be ringing the cash registers for you. It is paramount that not only the technical side of how to cook a pizza or repair a transmission be taught, but also that those trainees be mentally conditioned for all the other situations they will encounter. I guess you first have to decide whether you operate a Theory X or a Theory Y type of company and if you want to keep on that way. I am sure I need not go into a explanation of the two, since so much has been written and discussed about these terms in the last fifteen years. Once you decide whether you want to operate your X company like a Marine Corps general or to operate as a Y-type CEO who leads his people to want to produce, then your training philosophy can be established.

Whether your franchise operations are owner operated or absentee owner operated, determines the types of classes you need to establish. With either type, I have found it very important to get all of them in for owners' orientation classes. This prevents a lot of heartache later on. They must understand how and, above all, why things are done the way they are. If they are absentee owners, they must be taught the pitfalls of absenteeism and how to institute controls. Their psyches must be tuned in so cooperation is obtained for the life of the franchise. Yes, they must be brainwashed, but be sure it is correct, honest, and not overstated. That can kill you. It is very necessary not to blow smoke at them. Likewise, be sure to tell them all the bad things to expect and where your weaknesses are. They do not expect you to be perfect. If they are forewarned, the pitfalls will not seem as deep should they fall into one. If you do this orientation well, you can save or earn a lot of money in your future.

I have seen members of sales and training departments who knew where the problem spots were with their company, then maneuvered around them so as not to shake the new or potential franchisee. That tactic is wrong and will cause you problems later, for the franchisee will find them anyway. When he does, your evasiveness is one more thing heaped upon the fire. One day you hear a knock on your door and there he stands with three others who say they represent a majority if your franchisees. They call themselves Franchisees for Reform. They are the reformers and you are the reformee. Next you learn that two of these fellows are out in left field most of the time and are not even slightly rational in their thinking. Yet this is the group you must negotiate with for your survival.

HOW TO START OFF EVERYONE CORRECTLY

In the beginning your departments told franchisees it never rained on Fridays. It is so much easier to tell them it rains on some Fridays. Friday is usually their best sales day. The rain will wash out business on that day, and so forth. A year later, when it rains four Fridays in a row, they will not rise up against you but instead will think, "Boy, have I been fortunate. The company told me it would rain on some Fridays and this is the first time it has in the year I've been in business."

You will never have them in a better frame of mind to hear and believe you than in that initial training class when they are new and green. Later, they will have become "experts" in your business and be telling you how things should be run. It is like the Catholic girl who started dating a Protestant boy and fell in love with him. A few months later she came home crying and her mother asked what was the matter. She said it was evident that since she was Catholic and he Protestant, they could never be married. Her mother, being very wise, suggested she sell him on becoming Catholic; she reminded her daughter, "He will never be in a better mood to buy than he is now."

It is the same with a franchisee. In this early stage of your relationship the franchisee is in the best listening, hearing, and believing mood he will ever be in. Just be sure that what you are telling him is honest, true, factual, and all of those good words. (P.S. The outcome of the Catholic girl story was that she came home a few weeks later very happy. She told her mother it had worked—she had convinced him to become a Catholic. Then after a few months she came home crying again. Her mother asked what had happened. She said she had oversold him...and he was becoming a priest! There is another moral there.)

To be sure the right information is coming out of the training department, tape everything at least once a year and listen to it. I know, you say that it is a seven-day-a-week class for three weeks and you can't take the time. Well, it can take more than three weeks of your time to fight the battles later. There is a shortcut. I purchased one of those variable-speed cassette tape recorder/players. I plug it into the cigarette lighter in my car and set the speed on double time, which plays it back twice as fast as it was recorded. It works with special electronic circuits so you can understand it and cuts the listening time in half. Every time I get in the car I listen to it until I have heard it all. I make notes on a small mini-cassette dictator about anything that needs changing. You will hear plenty to be changed, even if it is the same trainer each year. A lot will be good, positive changes about things you have learned since last year which improve overall performance.

PLEASE DO NOT CUT TRAINING SHORT!

Another warning: Do not cut short the training budget. You spend hundreds of thousands of dollars on buildings, marketing research, and the product itself. Then you make training squeak by with holes in the filmstrips. You have priorities in the wrong place, my friend. Think about yourself. Where would you be without training, whether you were trained by your parents, grandparents, friends, schoolteachers, fellow workers, O.J.T., or just plain self-taught by books. Sure, there are different types, but it is all training and it all serves a purpose. That is the key: *purpose*. What is the ultimate, bottom line purpose of your training? Go beyond the obvious and get to that bottom line. Well, look now at your business budget priorities. You cannot rationalize by saying "I have a superior product or professional service and therefore things/business will come to us" or "we are busting our seams now." If that should be true, then your growth can be tripled if you have the proper support services for that super-duper product or service.

People, properly trained in the psychological as well as physical side of the business, are assets that will spread your balance sheet well. It is a return on investment (ROI) which I have never seen on the books of any company, but one which is a very real asset. Training can actually make the difference between staying in business or going out.

Depending on your type of operation, but especially in the case of owner-operators, the training school may be one of the best (perhaps last, also) places to wash a franchisee out of your program. Let's say the potential franchisee has passed the initial sales steps, he has passed the psychological tests, he has passed the financial hurdles, he has been approved, and now he is in the training class. The instructor will get to know him pretty well. If he sees that someone is not suited for your type of business, you had better take another look. This could be an opportunity to perform a valuable service to both parties—to the franchisee because he is possibly laying his future, his family's future, and his wordly possessions on the line. If you can prevent trouble, do so. Don't let greed take over. You remember "Do unto others...." It is the right thing to do even if you aren't a religious person.

The other reason is for your company's benefit. If this fellow were just right for your business and would be very successful, no problem. He would probably open twenty-five more franchised units for you. But one who is not successful usually looks to blame it on someone else. And who is the one who is supposed to have told him all the right ways to succeed? Who is the one who said he knew all the correct answers? Who is the one he paid to teach him how to make money in this business? Why you, the franchisor, of course! So if you did not teach him all those things correctly, then whose fault is it? Yours! Now he feels like punching the fat, happy, wealthy franchisor in the nose. Physically doing that may be a problem, but he can legally try, and he may be repaid for all his money, time, effort, tears, divorce, and so on that you cause him. Even if you win the case, the cost of legal assistance, executive and sales time will be a loss. Get this guy out before he gets started. Not only does it serve him but you as well.

Next, make that training class enthusiastic. People love to be stimulated. You think they just want hard, cold facts? Try this. Have you ever been in a class, half asleep, slouching in the chair, and suddenly a gorgeous, shapely, sensuous, femme fatale walks in and stands there for a few minutes as she surveys the room looking for a seat. She then comes over and sits down next to you, crosses her legs, glances over at you, and smiles a pleasant "hello" type of smile.

Were you stimulated? Did you enjoy it? Was that a more enjoyable class from then on? Okay, then see that the training class is stimulating, enthusiastic, exciting, challenging, dynamic, and honest. People like to talk about new and exciting experiences. If your classes are stimulating, your new "goodwill salespeople" are producing for you even before class is out.

HOW TO SCREEN FOR GOOD PEOPLE

How about interviews to screen potential franchisees? Some companies have the sales department do it, some have the training department do it, while others have a separate department. It depends on your size, the number of people coming to you, and the desired depth of the process. Perhaps you have a franchise system where your owners are merely passive investors. Your primary job of training becomes one of screening managers and processing them through your school. How do you pick the best; how do you anticipate the ones who will be short-timers in your business? I worked on this problem with one franchisor, and in the first year there was a 36 percent drop in turnover when the proper questions were asked up front.

First we took a cross section of good managers and established a personality profile on them. Next we did the same on poor managers or those who were fired or quit. Then we did one on the middle-of-the-road managers. After evaluating these, we found each of the three groups had certain qualities and faults. We merely isolated the good qualities of the successful managers and started hiring only those who matched up. It sounds simple, but actually it was a technical psychological process we were working with. The important thing is, it worked.

It doesn't matter whether it is a file clerk or a department head. Many who hire others do not do a very proficient job. I think the reasons are because it is not done often and it seems like the job should be simple. Therefore, the scientific criteria are not considered top priority. Yet when you add years of on-the-job salary for that person, and consider the thousands of dollars his decisions will usually affect, these criteria are important. Take the time to learn to hire people professionally.

Then put everyone who comes to work for you, through your manager and/or owner, training classes. You read that right—everyone! Your file clerks, your secretaries, department heads, vice presidents, and you, too—everyone. It will make or save you a lot of money. When I was actively running our franchising company, I decided to take a ninety-day period and see that everyone got some actual on-the-job training in one of our units. There was a lot of squawking about not having time to do it, but everyone went. After the first few came back to the main office, there was no more complaining from anyone about going. They came back charged up about what they had seen and done on the job. They had loads of ideas for changes, ideas for marketing, product and service changes, customer relations, franchisee relations, everything you can think of, and it was all presented positively.

There were other benefits. When a franchisee or manager called in from the field with a problem, the secretary often handled it without it ever going to the supervisor or department head. She could do this because she understood the problem from having been in the field herself. There was also a lot of sympathy created. Thus our home office people cooperated more with each other and with the field people; above all, they cooperated faster for quick solutions.

Lastly, our home office people felt more a part of the family. They had more knowledgeable input; more second- and third-level people above them listened to their thoughts. Good egos were properly fed and everyone was happier.

The training and personnel departments will often be one or closely affiliated with each other. Thus, not only managers for company or franchisee units will be hired there, but also home office managers or potential manager types. Since the screening process is so important, it will save you money all the way around to have it done by someone who is well trained.

28

The Operations Department

It Is Necessary to Control for Profits

I would rather attempt to do something great and fail than attempt to do nothing and succeed.

One day several years ago I was in a store that was rather busy. There were three or four customers ahead of me. I watched a rather curt young sales clerk do them a favor by waiting on them. When my turn came she began to give me the same treatment. I looked at her and said, "I think you have the situation here a little mixed up. You see, you are the overhead here, I am profit." She looked up at me rather startled and said, "What does that mean?" There we have one of the great problems of business today.

The people who are in contact with the buying customer, the people who ring the cash register, have not been trained in why and how the system is supposed to work. Yet explaining it to them can be simple: Just explain who is overhead and who is profit.

Under a capitalistic free enterprise system of economics, no one holds a gun to anyone's head and says "You must buy from me." He who best serves the customer's desire gets the business. To a large extent, serving the customer falls under the assistance and guidance of the operations department. The good business person appreciates his dependence upon the public. He realizes he can reach his potential in profits only when he can develop a sense of self-worth and an attitude of service rather than servitude. Firing an offending employee does not necessarily solve the problem. One must analyze the causes rather than the symptoms, the true feelings rather than the actions.

HOW TO DESIGN YOUR OPERATIONS MANUAL

I realize it is hard to put four years of psycholgy into an operations manual, but I think there should be a chapter, in sixth-grade language, on some of the main thoughts on psychology as it applies to your types of business. In fact, it should probably be the first chapter.

Your operations manual should be one of the first things you develop, for it will be one of your most important tools. It should cover everything! Now that is an all-inclusive statement. It was meant to be. Every step a franchisee operation will take should be in there. Start with what takes place after the franchisee is approved by your licensing committee. Set up checklists so he will miss nothing. Go through rules and regulations, quality control procedures, and the duties of every single person in the entire operation, by category. Cover every administrative function; all about employees, from recruiting to firing; maintenance; safety; sales methods; banking; and on and on. There should be nothing any employee or franchise could ask that is not "in the book."

Naturally, this should be the Bible of the training department and every other department as it applies to running a unit and coordination with field operations and franchisees. You may want to break the operations manual into department sections such as accounting, marketing, and so on, and have those departments author their own sections.

You may need two operations manuals, one for the actual on-the-job manager and perhaps one for the owner. There would not be much overlap in the two manuals. There are obvious things the owner should know that should not concern the manager. While the owner would have both the operations manual and the owner's manual, the manager would need only the former. If it is an owner/manager situation, then one person would get both.

DEVELOPING A FIELD INSPECTOR

The operations department is responsible for field inspections, checking to see that everything complies with your methods and quality of operation. Usually, those inspectors act as troubleshooters in helping the units improve where needed. At times of emergency, they may even fill in as operating managers.

These inspector/consultants must be leaders. They must know how to handle every situation. A good leader is someone who knows the way, shows the way, and goes the way himself. Therefore, it is imperative that he come up through the ranks of experience. This valuable hands-on learning experience is worth a lot to those he counsels and thus to you. Be extremely careful when you hire an inspector. Judge well; hire accordingly; pay well. To every franchisee the inspector/consultant represents you, your ideals, ideas, desires, methods, and above all, how you feel about them. These attitudes are conveyed through your field people. In addition, much of the success of many franchisees depends on the inspector/consultant's intelligence and his ability to communicate well.

Since people have different abilities, it is wise to transfer these inspector/consultants into different territories occasionally, even if it is only temporary. This will help your system as well as assist in protecting its integrity. Occasionally everyone becomes complacent and lets things slide. Check the inspection reports carefully; you will see how transferring helps.

Some companies I have done consulting for use the big-brother concept. Through an understanding with the franchisees, when a new franchisee comes on line, an older franchisee near him is assigned as his big brother. He assists the new franchisee, mostly from the other end of the telephone, with questions that are particular to their area. Often, this help blends into all operational areas. Usually, warm friendships develop. As time progresses, the benefits flow both ways: The learning experience of the new and purer-thinking franchisee becomes valuable to the older franchisee and, in turn, to the whole system.

Be careful in attempting this big-brother program. I have seen similar situations backfire when the old franchisee had his own ideas about how everything should be done, and they were not the same as the franchisor. The program can be very good, but it must be carefully planned and executed.

In almost every type of franchise system, the operations department should be involved in the planning and implementation of most changes that take place. The interlacing between departments when change is being contemplated almost always involves operations.

What type of upgrading and ongoing training will operations conduct for owners, managers, or others? How will they handle locations that show less than satisfactory performance? How will they direct the training stores in the field if this is one of your methods? How do they handle a franchisee who doesn't go by "your book"? Exactly what latitude does operations have? The list goes on.

How often should you inspect? Should your inspectors announce their appearance ahead of time? There are many who say yes because it is unfair to just drop in, but it should not matter. If you have customers daily, then the operation should run fully complying with all standards at all times, so it would make no difference when the inspector came by, announced or unannounced. Some say it is better to let the franchisee know so he can get ready. My answer is the same as before. Does every customer notify you ahead so you can get ready? If that is the way you operate, would you get ready for the customer the same way you do the inspector? Obviously not!

Never tell the unit in advance that the inspector is coming. Whether he is there or not should have no effect on the standards, dress, service, attitudes, or anything else. The inspector is just another customer, and he is viewing, grading, and judging the same things customers do. The difference is that he is going behind the scenes to check those things that make the product and service come out like it is supposed to. Then he will case his vote for all to see. When the inspector does this, he helps you; the customer doesn't. If the customer doesn't like his treatment, he votes with his feet and walks out—usually not telling anyone except his friends.

A camera is an especially good tool for an inspector. When you preserve a situation for posterity in living color, it is much more impressive as far as getting it corrected. It also becomes a good tool should you ever need one in enforcing your requirements legally. Be sure to have your inspector put the date, time, exact location, and sign his name on the back of the photo.

HOW MUCH IS ENOUGH QUALITY CONTROL?

How much is enough? If you are talking about earnings or love, that will probably differ with each individual, but when it comes to quality control of your franchised unit, it is not so nebulous. You can and must establish exact policies. This doesn't mean good judgment will not bend or change these policies as you grow or as time passes. It does mean that your people and your franchisees will know exactly where they stand. If a franchisee does not pass inspection, perhaps he receives a warning and is reinspected in two weeks. He may even be charged for the cost of reinspection. If he passes the second time or significant progress has been made, you may allow him to continue and check again. You establish the rules from the standpoint of your need.

Just remember that the control of your system quality and standards are the lead defense in protecting your logo, trademarks, and service marks. Accumulate the necessary documentation as you go. It may become very important, if lawyers get involved. I am not saying this from a negative view of franchisees; I am merely saying you must protect the system or you will possibly lose it. You must protect the system for the benefit of all your other franchisees. One or two who do not comply will hurt your name, and it is your name the other franchisees are also using. Protect everyone by establishing fair, obtainable, profitable standards.

29

The Accounting Department

Why You Need Good Numbers To Be a Money-Making Organization

The most dangerous thing in the world is a negative-thinking expert.

A few years back our company needed a new comptroller. I asked the accounting firm that certified our books each year to do the screening for me and pick the top three so I could make a decision. When the screening was over, the three contenders came in for interviews. I asked many of the usual questions, but there was one unusual one. At the conclusion of each interview I would ask, "How much is two plus two?" The first two applicants each thought I was kidding. When I assured them I was not, they each answered "four." The last contender looked at me with a sober expression on his face and said, "What do you want it to equal?" I'll see if I can legitimately make it come out that way." I hired him!

That type of creative mind is an unusual trait for people who are taught always to think in the analytical and absolute. Yet it is extremely valuable in today's complicated Internal Revenue, Securities Exchange Commission, Federal Trade Commission, and franchise-related world. I am certainly not suggesting dishonesty. I am merely saying the person who can think through the regulations to multitier corporate structures for better tax benefits or who can design creative financing with the best leverage possible is a real asset and an unusual one for the accounting field.

HOW TO KNOW WHAT DECISIONS TO ASK FOR

There is another reason to seek out this type of person. Many negative-thinking experts in the accounting and legal fields have killed numerous

148

good deals. They are automatically elevated to the expert status by the complexity of their professions, and we have a tendency to respect their opinions as godlike foresight. And rightfully so...as long as the opinions are restricted to their professions and not extended to the area of business management.

Years ago I made a request of the CPA who handles my personal tax work. I asked him to assist me in making all the right moves in connection with taxes and never give me advice on whether a decision or business deal was good or bad. I would make the business decisions and he would make the tax decisions. It has worked extremely well.

When a specialist in law, accounting, marketing, construction, or any technical field starts telling you whether or not to make a deal based on anything other than their specific area of expertise, you need to correct the situation or make a change in whom you consult.

HOW TO ESTABLISH YOUR BUDGET

One of the first things the accounting department must do is establish your budgets. Every department must know what its perimeters are. Goals are rarely reached if they are not formally set. Conversely, expense limits are almost always reached or exceeded whether set or not. You would be amazed to know how many businesses operate without formal, written numbers. Human nature does not perform at its best under those circumstances. In order to set up the budget, you need a chart of accounts. Get every department in on this act. They can tell you numerous categories for your chart, which are necessary to give everyone the information they need.

Actually, you will be setting up two charts of account, one for the franchisee and company-owned outlets and one for your operation as franchisor. When designing the chart and related forms to be used by the franchisees, be sure to outline the purpose of the system first. Those requirements will help you eliminate a lot of unnecessary accounting work. Often we have a tendency to overcontrol and require infomation we do not use. Note I did not say "need," I said "use." There is a difference. If you are not using it, if its purpose is not being followed through to conclusion, then do not put others through the trouble of acquiring the information.

On the other hand, plot the purpose well enough to get all the information you need for monitoring, control, foresight, planning, and making profits. To get information from franchisees, you need properly to cover same in the license agreement and otherwise explain its purpose. If the purpose is logical, you generally will not meet resistance. If it makes no sense, the franchisees will resist you and will not take the time to keep the extra information coming to you. Worse yet, they may then omit some of the pertinent data you use or they may treat it so laxly it will be incorrect.

Information properly put to timely use can serve as a radar system, giving you early warning of possible trouble ahead. Once you have trends established, you can save plenty by observing them and taking action before any difficulty entrenches itself.

Just as operations has checks to determine if all moneys are being accounted for, the accounting department should have backups to determine the same thing. Are certain expenses rationing out properly with sales and all of the other checks you can develop? Above all, are you getting your property royalty fee based on honest figures?

You might start with a chart of accounts that is standard for your particular industry. Then make the necessary modifications your company needs. By not varying greatly, you have the advantage of industrywise comparison.

HOW TO SERVE THE FRANCHISEE UNIFORMLY

Be sure the system you design for the franchisee is uniformly enforced in your license agreement. You want everyone reporting go you the same way. If you do not have this uniformity, the numbers become meaningless from a comparison standpoint and there goes part of your control, planning, and radar system.

You may want to set up your home office system so you can offer partial or complete bookkeeping and accounting services through your accounting department. You can charge for this service and make a very nice profit. There is a good likelihood you can perform these services on your computer at a lesser cost than the franchisee can obtain the service locally. After all, you are already programmed and on the exact format for your company outlets. If you do not want to do this, you may find it worthwhile to check into companies who perform these services for small businesses, like General Business Services or Comprehensive Accounting. They both have hundreds of local offices all over the United States.

HOW TO CUT BACK ON PAPERWORK

Paperwork costs everybody money. How do you do without it? The answer is you don't, but you can cut it back. Every six months I recommend that your people take a planned, formal look at what can be eliminated, combined, or redesigned. This not only goes for your franchisor office, but for those outlets in the field. Store managers and owners will love you for this attack on detested paperwork.

One of the easiest ways to accomplish this is to ask everybody for suggestions, Remember, each time you ask for information or assistance, you must follow through and advise those who helped as to the outcome, otherwise you will gain a reputation for giving lip service toward problems. The simplest ideas will come in. You will scratch your head at how obvious some of them are, and yet no one ever got around to thinking or doing anything about it until now. An asset of this kind of problem solving is that it makes everybody feel important to the overall effort... and they are.

Caution: Do not let reporting from the field lag. That can cause snarl-ups in other areas. It also may be one of those warning signs that there is trouble in River City. Check it out fast and let the licensee know you are on top of things. He may need help, he may be holding back, or maybe someone just forgot.

The type of cash register or accounting equipment you recommend needs more than just a casual investigation. Do not get your people locked into using equipment that only does two-thirds of the job. At the same time, the state of the art is changing so fast, be sure your choice is as compatible as possible with the other processes it must tie into. In addition, check out what future designs seem to be on the horizon. Is what you have chosen at least partially compatible with the new equipment that will be available five years from now?

Another caution: The Sherman Antitrust Act and related regulations have far-reaching tentacles. You might be considered in violation if you require your licensees to buy a certain specific brand of equipment. You can certainly recommend and state what type of record information must be kept. The exception might be something like a computerized cash register which reports to your home office computer by telephone line at the end of each day. This equipment must be compatible with yours. Another might be a motel chain that has computerized reservations going in and out of their motels. Your franchise attorney should check out your thoughts in this area before you do anything.

Be sure each department in your organization is set up as a profit center from day one. I know each will not have income and thus cannot be a profit center in the exact sense of the word, but they can all be under allocated budgets and operate for maximum efficiency and production. This control will be well worth the effort.

COMPUTERS AND MANPOWER

What about home office computers? I think the proper answer to that question would have to be, What about computers? No one seems to know totally. The important word there is "totally." Every computer sales company will tell you all about the wonderful things they have and what they can do. The key word here is "can." What they can do and what they will do for you are sometimes different.

First, do not expect to eliminate much of your existing manpower with a computer. I have yet to see one that did much in that respect. Next, be prepared for the programming to cost you at least what the computer did, or perhaps twice as much. Then be prepared for it to take you from three to four times as long to get it programmed and debugged as the salesman or programmer tells you.

A smart up-front move is to hire someone highly qualified in computers. When you get ready to hire your computer specialist, contract your accounting firm (if they are sharp on computers) to screen him for you. This is because you probably do not have the expertise to know what you are doing. Even if you knew last year, that knowledge is outdated today. People in technical fields can sell you so logically and sincerely that you may hire the wrong person—not that he was dishonest, but he knows what he knows. You need to have your representative (accounting firm), who knows what you need, find someone who matches that need. You probably do not know what your in-depth needs will be and certainly cannot handle the highly technical language, which explodes with new ideas and buzzwords every month.

Should you buy, lease, or what? There are dozens of advantages on all sides. Much depends on your size (volume) now and in the near future. If you buy, what you have will be outdated in five years. There is a market for used equipment, but obsolete equipment means a big drop in what you get for it...and it will be at least somewhat obsolete. This is one question where all of your facts need to be weighed.

One small franchisor I consulted with made the decision just to put in terminals with screens and printers. He tied in by telephone line to the huge computers at the local bank who sold time on their machines as a separate profit center. They even did minor programming to meet his specific needs. One good point was that almost all of his needs were already programmed into the computers. He had to pay for very little in that area. The bank had high-speed printers which printed thirteen times faster than the ones in his office, so he had the bank do almost all the printing from its machine. That saved thirteen times the hourly rate. On top of that, they printed after midnight, when the hourly rate was cut in half. That produced a cost ratio of 26 to 1. The bank had its own messenger deliver the copy to the nearby branch the next morning, and the company just picked it up when someone went to the bank to make a deposit. They saved about 52 percent of what it would have cost ot install, program, and produce hard copy on their own unit. The big pluses were no purchase investment and no obsolete equipment in five years.

30

The Marketing Department

How to Let This Department Take Over Your Company...and Make You Rich

> *You can fool some of the people some of the time (and a lot of people think that is enough).*

Some people think it is the marketing department's job to draw up beautiful ads that attract people no matter what you say or show in the ad. Fooling people to get them in our outlet is not how a lasting business is built. I am firmly convinced that marketing talent can cut your climb to success in half, prolong it to infinity, or navigate it to destruction.

A few years ago I met a man for the first time, and during our conversation he asked what business I was in. I told him I was in the marketing business. "The way I see it, I am driving a marketing truck that just happens to have Motels and Hotels written on the side." That is the way I still see it today. The fact that I was in the motel and hotel business is secondary. If nothing gets marketed, then I would not be in business—at least not for very long.

THE ONLY BUSINESS YOU'RE IN IS THE MARKETING BUSINESS

We are all in the marketing business first and foremost. I'm sure most readers will agree, but the problem is you agree here and forget it by tomorrow—or at least you need to be reminded so you consistently can be alert to this fact. Literally every day something takes place that would be positive for marketing to release to the media. It takes training of the mind to become aware of these things. Once you learn how, you can get hundreds of thousands of dollars worth of advertising free!

I did say free, and that brings me to public relations (PR). It is so easy if you know how. The first two-and-one-half years after we started our company, our paid advertising amounted to less than twenty-five dollars. We had thousands of dollars worth of free PR. Think about the psychology of people and their jobs, the people who put out newspapers and magazines and those who run TV and radio news programs. They have constant deadlines to meet, many of them daily. It is a lot of work.

Let's take the newspaper as an example. They have to come up with stories to fill that paper every day. Suppose you were to write a story or short item in proper form, take the proper size black-and-white glossy photos, and deliver it all to the proper editor. His job is easy: Edit and print. That is the way it can happen very often.

HOW TO SMELL OUT FREE STORIES

The story cannot be just any story. Any good marketing/PR person knows how to smell out a worthy idea and put it in proper form to get it published. It is not just smelling; often it is creative dreaming. I'll give you an example.

A few years back I wanted to get a free story in the newspaper to keep our name in front of the public and continue to make people think what a nice place our motels were. It was around the first of December. I pondered for a while, and shortly an idea came. Next, I related it to the marketing department so they could write the story for the newspapers. The motel managers were sent copies of the story with instructions for getting a photographer, hiring a Santa Claus, buying twenty-five presents for small children, and getting three high school boys with a car.

Here is how it all went. The Saturday before Christmas, Santa Claus was stationed by the side of the road in front of the motel. He was waving at the people driving by. A car pulled up alongside him; two teenage boys jumped out of the backseat, grabbed Santa, and pushed him and his bag of toys into the car. All of this was caught on film by the photographer who was standing nearby. The car sped off. The teenagers took Santa and the gifts to the children's ward of a local hospital, where Santa brought gifts and joy to those small patients. Again, this was captured on film by the photographer.

The film was printed immediately; the story and photos were turned over to the newspaper, radio, and TV news editors later that afternoon. That night we made the newscasts, and the next morning we were on the bottom half of the front page with pictures and a bold byline that said, "Santa Claus kidnapped on U.S. #50." The story praised the owners of the motel for their civic pride in doing something in such a unique way for the hospitalized children at Christmas. They ran the story almost exactly as we had written it. That type of PR was worth ten times what the same amount of space in a paid ad would have done for us.

Another instance was when we put in a new generation of computers at the home office. We took a picture of several accounting people standing around the computer with frowns on their faces. The headline on the story was "Computers Are Not So Smart." The story line was built around all of the fantastic capabilities of this new computer, which cost thousands upon thousands of dollars, and how on its first trial run, when asked, "Who's buried in Grant's tomb?" it said it didn't know!

These various things cannot smell like paid advertising or the editors will never run them. They like human-interest items, items that have readership appeal, most and, definitely, stories that are already written with photos taken. This same type of story creation can be done with any medium to which potential franchisees or end-user customers subscribe.

If asked to define *public relations*, one might say it is the art or science of developing reciprocal understanding and goodwill between a person, firm, or institution and the public. To do this, the person in charge of PR must have a close relationship with all department heads and especially top management. How else could he find out about what is happening in the company so he can report or dream up a story for release. If he is not made aware of every little seemingly unimportant fact, you have lost some excellent free press.

YOUR PUBLIC RELATIONS GUIDE

For members of IFA, the association puts out a booklet called "The Franchisor's Guide to Public Relations." I will not attempt to rewrite that brochure, but I shall convey some of the ideas. What does PR do for your company and is it worth the effort? I'll comment on a few things here; you be the judge.

First, there are various types of PR: PR with your franchisees, PR with the general customer public, PR with stockholders, PR with employees, PR with suppliers and just about everyone. PR can build a better image with each one of these groups, depending in how it is aimed.

You have heard it said that word of mouth is the best advertising. True, but it is properly referred to if you label that "word of mouth" PR. It brings customers to your outlets, it sells more franchises, it convinces financial institutions to make loans, it persuades suppliers to extend credit, and on and on. PR is that third person talking, it's that "word of mouth" talking for you, about you. It is not viewed as a paid-for ad. It is considered much, much more factual because that independent third party is saying it.

A good PR person can help take the heat off if something bad happens. He can be prepared properly in advance. He can quickly and intelligently communicate with the press and thus the public. He will never hide. He will be honest with the facts; face the problems squarely, professionally, and honesty; and the public will forgive and forget. Hide or dance around the problem or accusations and the public will take an adversary position against you.

PR assists you in getting the maximum benefit from any contributions you make toward your community, whether in time, money, or goods. It helps you to get your money's worth, so to speak. It also assists in motivating your employees to help out in the community. Then they will feel good about themselves, the community will like them and you more, sales will go up—everyone benefits. PR includes close attention to your employees' accomplishments. Deserving employees who are praised in the press and in-house publications appreciate the attention. They become better employees. Old products can be repositioned in the marketplace with good PR. New products can be given push with proper PR. They can be romanced to success.

There are no limits. A good staff in this area of your company can pay their costs ten to one hundred times a year. They can build your sales in giant steps. It is a very important department. PR, marketing, advertising—they all are words that often get thrown together by most business people. More often than not, only those who have trained in one or all three fields know the technical difference. Regardless of the fine points, the goal is to convey an idea that will result in a sale.

HOW TO ELIMINATE THE NEED TO SELL

At the same time, I guess I would have to say the ideal would be to eliminate selling. The ultimate would really be to have your PR, marketing, and advertising departments be so good, so well tuned, as to make the need for selling unnecessary. To do this, you would have to understand the customer precisely, then design your product or service accordingly, and thus it would sell itself. You would then make your wares available and that would be all there is to it. There you have the ideal.

Often things get started just the other way around. We design a product first, then try to market it to the public. Sometimes this works. In addition, occasionally we can create a need the public didn't know they had. Do your homework. Statistics, logistics, demographics, and all the rest are vital for maximum success in a minimum of time. Never stop!

McDonald's is one highly successful operation, I'm sure everyone will agree. Look at the changes in decor, menu, product—it never stops. They test-sample until the statistics confuse the statisticians. They test the tests. Those folks can tell you what needs are to be met before they become needs; and then they fill those needs.

Keeping customers happy is not a new tactic by any means, but to approach every move scientifically is new to many businesses. The old philosophy of doing things the same way because it always worked in the past is not good enough anymore. The marketing department should be in charge of almost everything. They should know what the customer wants, what he will pay, where he wants it, when he wants it, what colors he wants, how high and how long he wants it, and how many he wants. Therefore, they should establish the product, the price, the production, inventory, sales techniques, and service requirements and methods. Sound crazy? Think about it! Read it over again. As I said before, you are driving a marketing truck. It just happens to have Motels, Hamburgers, Accounting Services, or Bicycles written on the side of it.

You must view your business as a customer-satisfying organization and not a product- or service-producing company. That is secondary. Satisfy the customer first. If there is no need, then there is no consumer to be satisfied unless perhaps you are in a business where a new desire can be created. Then sales may be made not out of need, but merely out of want.

WHAT ABOUT ADVERTISING AGENCIES?

Now we come to the question of using an agency. There are many points for and against agencies. Since their services do not comprise an exact science, but rather a personal service, it is tough to blueprint a plan. Since advertising is a personal service, I believe the prime consideration is the individual handling your account.

I have worked with large national agencies and small local agencies.

In each case, it is the account executive that makes the difference. There are some considerations that should be given to the information and staff that individual has behind him. Usually, I have found the big staff, and so on, which most large agencies try to sell you on, are overrated. A lot depends on how large you are and what you have to do. Generally, my comments herein are not directed to the giant franchisor. Their needs and requirements are different.

When I say it is the individual account executive who is important, I mean how experienced he is, how creative and how much loyalty and concentration he will give you. If he has experience working with exact or similar accounts to yours, that is a big plus. This means he has developed knowledge of the dos and don'ts for your industry—that is, someone else has paid for his schooling. You become the beneficiary.

HOW TO BE CREATIVE

Eric Fromm, a brilliant psychiatrist, once asked, "What are the conditions of the creative attitude, or seeing and responding, of being aware and sensitive to what one is aware of? First of all, it requires the capacity to be puzzled. Children still have the capacity to be puzzled, but once they are through the process of education, most people give up a large portion of the capacity of wondering—of being surprised. They feel they ought to know everything, and hence it is a sign of ignorance to be surprised or puzzled by anything."

Creativity, dreaming the new and different, is the valuable tool of great idea makers. The creative potion you mix up today will be the cure for tomorrow's problems. If that agency man can design a unique slogan, ad, TV spot, promotion, or point-of-purchase sales piece that works, then go with him. Remember, creating is not an original pattern, it is a combination of patterns and nothing more. There are millions of different patterns, and millions more will be created.

Nothing is really new, yet everything is new. New means taking existing elements that are available to everyone and arranging them so they are new to us or, especially, to the customer. Dare to dream and create; hire no one who cannot. The limits of creativity are set by those who can see only the ordinary. We impose limits or allow no limits—it is a conscious decision. Choose a person rather than choosing an agency. Listen to all his outlandish and wild ideas as long as he is wise in his common sense approach to the marketplace, its need, and its desires.

WAYS TO WORK WITH AD AGENCIES

Once you choose, there are some ground rules (all of which sometimes must be ignored) for working with agency people. First, once you go with a campaign, do just that: Go. The time to question is not when you are weeks or months into the campaign, that is, unless it is flopping miserably. Generally the time to question is three to six months before the campaign starts. Don't push for drastic changes if you have a campaign that is working. Stay with it until every man, woman, and child in the free world is sick of it. Then keep right on if it is working well.

Second, avoid temptation and don't take your own surveys. Mothers and spouses are great for curing colds, remembering birthdays, and thousands of other things, but avoid them for your personal advertising surveys. If they do not own the company, pay no attention to them. The only things that make a difference are facts, and that means numbers by the bushel. If someone says, "I can't stand...," or "My wife says...," then you know he or she knows nothing. Stay away from that person—he or she is not a professional.

Third, stay out of the copywriting business unless you want to change jobs. If you can write better than your agency, then you should either change jobs or fire the agency you have. This does not mean you should not feed the agency with your thoughts, but be careful. Unless you are working with someone who has a good amount of self-worth, he or she will use your ideas just to please you. If he or she generally does that, then you should fire him or her and get someone who is good and will stand up to you. If your agency produces for you, then stay out of their business until they fail. The person who freely controls the pen that writes the copy is very important. At the same time, if it is definitely not what you want and sales show the advertising is weak, then you are the boss.

Number four has to do with the ethics and legality of your advertising. Agencies have to understand that you must process some ads through the legal department. If legalities require it, then the advertising aces must use their creativity to say it legally. Just because their pride of authorship hurts is no reason to get in trouble. The same goes for ethics in advertising. You know what should not be said or implied. If you are not sure, change it; listen to that little voice. When in doubt, change. You can produce enough good ads without risking public rejection, associational ridicule, legal questioning, or just plain embarrassment.

Number five seems simple. Your vast knowledge of your product or service can work against you. Take all possibility of misunderstanding out of the information passed to your agency. This is especially true when you start with them. You know everything so well you probably use buzzwords and sometimes generalize. The agency must learn exactly and, above all, truly understand the intent of what you are saying. Break it down so they may comprehend clearly and become an extension of your knowledge.

Number six is to have your goals set down in writing. Match goals with amounts to be spent to produce them. Then let the agency figure out how best to spend it where. Sure, they need to give you a report back for your approval, but just because you or your spouse always read the movie page of the newspaper does not mean that is the best place to put your ads or even that your favorite newspaper is right at all. Let the professionals do their job. If they don't, get someone else.

Seven says, Seeing is understanding and understanding produces results. If you sell garden equipment, insist that the agency account executive get out in the backyard and try out the mowers, tractors, and all the other equipment. Then put him in a store for a few days so he can see how the shop runs. Next, send him to your operations department to experience some of their good and bad situations. After that he will understand, write better ads, and produce better results. If he doesn't want to go through all this, you have the wrong agency. I know it is a headache for him. I know he has had 1,463 other accounts who handle garden equipment, but...he has a decision to make. Do it or lose your account. Nothing can replace O.J.T.; this especially includes someone as vital as that agency person who will be spending hundreds of thousands of dollars of your money.

You can fall behind the eight ball with number eight: Do not ask for second opinions. I presume the agency has done their statistics scientifically and thoroughly knows what is correct. Second opinions are excellent for someone who is going to be operated on and wants another doctor to check things out, but this is not the case in advertising unless the second opinion is from another specialist who has all the scientific data. Everybody has opinions, and the more daringly dynamic the ad campaign, the more invalid the opinion of your executive vice president who supervises your manufacturing operations. If you are as smart as you should be, go with the agency and trust your smarts. If you can't decide, then you may have other problems that need solving before you tackle advertising. If you don't have experience, that is another subject. In that case, stay out of it and delegate the responsibility to someone who does have experience.

Nine lives you probably do not have, so watch out for number nine. If the vice president of operations, the vice president of sales, and the legal counsel all happen to see the ad and like it, be careful. Something is probably wrong with it. I know I have said heretofore, "Do not ask their opinion." However, if they should see it and they all feel it is just right, it would scare me. To play it that safe probably means the ad will only be read by those who know you personally. The general public has been trained to go for sharp, well-placed, hit-the-spot ads. One that seems perfect to everybody on staff is probably a problem.

YOUR MARKETING PLAN—ELEMENTS TO CONSIDER

Now that we have the agency taken care of, let us go into the area of marketing. Here are some questions you need to answer about marketing: Exactly who is responsible for your company's marketing plan? Do you have formal plans? Can independent decisions be made? How much research and by whom is needed to back up decisions? Some elements of that plan you must decide about are:

1. What is the speed of penetration?
2. What are the geographic territories?
3. What is the amount of advertising support?
4. Should you use the clustering approach?
5. Should you use random expansion for outlets?
6. What logistical support will be offered?
7. What supply support will be given?
8. What are all phases of timing?
9. What are the checkpoints for measuring success?
10. To what extent will franchisees be involved in plan formulation?
11. How is the plan initially communicated to franchisees for maximum adherence?
12. How is the plan integrated with franchisees?
13. What is the turnaround plan for problem markets?
14. How, when, and by whom is the plan to be updated?
15. What contributions and arrangements do you make in connection with grand openings for franchisees? For company-owned units? In regard to cooperative effort?
16. What development, strategies, and tactics are franchisees responsible for?

17. What percentage must franchisees contribute to the unified national budget?
18. Who governs how that budget shall be expended?
19. What criteria govern special promotions?
20. Who puts together your advertising manual?

Now that you are in shape, don't forget the manual for the marketing department to give to all franchisees. It should have samples of every type of release they might want to make, a complete set of graphics with colors used for every sign, and so on—a step-by-step program for new franchisees that will take them through every possible phase of advertising, marketing, and PR. Be explicit about every detail; do not assume anything. Last, assign responsibility for updating this manual often.

HOW TO PUT YOUR BEST PERSONAL FACE FORWARD

Another important part of marketing is the appearance you put forth. You are the company. When you are asked to make a speech, it is your organization the audience sees in their mind's eye. Let's take a look at how you can come off as top-flight.

Many executives think because they have a big title they are important, eloquent, and smart; sometimes they think they have a winning way with all people. They think since they know all about their business, they can stand up and be informative and entertaining. They are usually wrong. There is a saying that for every speech given there are actually three speeches: the one planned, the one given, and the one the speaker wishes he had given. Note the first one was planned. I have spoken at conventions from Chicago to Tokyo and from Los Angeles to Amsterdam, and I can tell you it had best be planned. I have been on the platform with some of the greatest orators, the greatest after-dinner speakers, and the greatest entertainers. Not one of those who are really great ever goes without a plan. If you want to be good, get your act together ahead of time.

Some think their performance starts when they stand up and walk to the lectern. It actually starts the moment you get anywhere near anyone who will be in your audience. That could be at the airport where someone meets you or in the lot where you park your car. You start with a warm friendly smile to everyone you see. It goes with you into the hotel lobby and the reception...anywhere you might run into a member of your audience. The best idea is to meet and shake hands with everyone you can.

Do not lock yourself up in a small circle and stay there. Do not sit at the table and wait for people to come over. At the same time, be humble. If you are not careful, going around shaking hands can make you look like you think you are something special. Just be down-to-earth, shake hands, exchange a few words, or possibly a cute joke, and be more than a visiting guest speaker—be a real live, one-of-them person.

The purpose of all this is to create your own little cheering section. Those who have just met you or knew you prior want you to do well. They will help you. You are not a stranger trying to crack that first funny story, but are their friend—and don't we all laugh with our friends? Do not underestimate the value of even five or six acquaintances in a crowd of several hundred.

Recently, I watched this in action. There were five singers performing some songs they did both together and solo. One of the women had been shaking hands and meeting people at two tables up front just before the show started. First, each did a solo. She was the fourth. All had been good and the audience of about one hundred responded well. This particular woman was not quite as good as the others, and the song she had chosen was not the best, though she did a good job. The audience clapped, but those two tables up front really clapped hard. One fellow stood up and shouted, "More Jeannie, more!" A few other at the table shouted, "More!" The next thing you know, the applause picked up, and she went off with huge applause. Actually, she was not as good as the three before her, but she got the encore and the biggest applause. Big stars know that enthusiasm, applause, and laughter are catching. I'm sure you are familiar with the person who comes out to warm up the audience before the star appears. It works!

After you, Mr. Guest Speaker, have used the available moments shaking hands, it is now time to go sit at the head table. You are up there in plain view. The audience will be watching you through whatever activities are to take place; this may include a meal. They will get to watch you eat. At one time or another, every member of that assembly will look at you. The bigger a celebrity you are, the more looks you will attract. You are being evaluated and categorized before you ever get up to speak. That evaluation is important. Would you like you if you were in the audience looking at you?

You can win many now that you did not shake hands with. Don't sit there stone-faced, buried in notes, or not paying any attention to those in the audience, and especially those sitting next to you. If you act that way and then burst into smiles and charm the instant you stand up to speak, the audience will smell a phony. If you laugh at the other speakers' jokes, talk to your seatmate at dinner, clap when they clap, and just enjoy the world around you, then you are one of them. You are and must be "on stage," but try to appear comfortable. As you carry out these various actions you will gain something else—information. You will get items that you might sandwich into your speech. You will learn more about the organization. Look over the program, menu, anything in the room such as signs, banners, or special flower arrangements. Check out everything. Next, the introduction starts. Which one? Why, the one who had prepared and your secretary sent to the chairman. It is a copy of the same one you carry with you in case the postman lost it or the introducer misplaced it. This way you know the right things are being said. As you hear him start, you set your mind on the great success you are as a speaker. You can hear the applause, warmth, and true appreciation coming from the audience because you are good. Don't write this off; it does make a difference. Remember what the Bible says: "As a man thinketh, so is he." Think success, think greatness, and rise to the occasion. Dare to be great.

You rise and move carefully to the lectern. Do not pause to take a drink of water, test the mike, shuffle notes, or whatever. You move right off with vigor and greatness. Anything you have to do with the mike or notes, do it as if you did not realize you were doing anything, and keep rolling.

All your contacts will not be before large live audiences. Some will be small groups, a single reporter in your office, or perhaps a TV studio with only the interviewer and camera crew. Since appearance at every opportunity are important, perhaps I can pass along a few other ideas on communications in general.

STAYING ON TOP OF INTERVIEWS AND SPEECHES

Let's look at interviews. The first rule is, Do not let your answers happen by accident. Professional interviewers plan what they want to lead you into, so why shouldn't you plan what you want to answer and lead them into? At least attempt to preplan what they will probably hit you with; have logical, honest answers ready. If you are on TV and if you can insist on camera placement, you can help yourself again. If you want to look younger, have no close-ups. Distance shots will make you look eight to ten years younger.

Next, create whatever image you want to project to that TV audience. Wear middle-range colors, not light or dark, unless you want to create a special image. For instance, dark-colored suits give off a sophisticated image. Light-colored suits give off an uneducated, unaware image. If you always wear light-sensitive glasses that turn darker in bright light, they will do that under those TV lights. You will then come off with that gangster image. Likewise, dark glass frames will probably distort the image you want to project. An unshaven look or little blemishes come off badly also. No matter what the interviewer may suggest, get some face makeup. Get it one shade darker than your skin and put it over that five o'clock shadow (and blemishes), even if you shaved only thirty minutes prior. You want to look natural, and these things help you do just that.

Let's go back to those speeches again. If you are going a speech, make it only fifteen or twenty minutes long unless you are very, very good. If someone calls and insists on thirty minutes, tell them okay and do a maximum of twenty anyway. Have you ever heard people complain or just make a comment about someone talking a little too long? Certainly. Well, have you ever heard a complaint about anyone speaking for too short a time? You get the point!

If someone asks you to cut it short just before you stand up...do your fifteen to twenty minutes anyway. Do not cut out the center of your speech or you will probably mess up the flow of your message. If they have planned so poorly they need you to cut, don't do it. Better to get the message across and make sense than to mess it up and get blamed for someone else's mistake. The time problem will pass and be forgotten, but a screwed-up speech probably will not.

If you are going into an interview situation, be sure those answers you have prepared take only twenty or thirty seconds to give. First, that is the way interviewers like it. Second, if you take longer, it will work against you. After thirty seconds, you lose your directness toward the question. It will seem as though you don't know the answer or, worse yet, are trying to evade it.

There is another special reason for preparing answers ahead of time. If you know, you do not have to spend your time thinking and searching for the answer, which would make you seem less than brilliant. By knowing the answer in advance, you can think about how your expression and voice are coming across. Two or three days later, people will probably have forgotten the technicalities of your answer, but the impression of how sincere you seemed and sounded will still be in their minds. How you seem to the public is very important. Be careful, and don't allow yourself to be baited. If the interviewer gets loud or curt, the natural reaction is to come back the same way and show him who is boss. If you do that, you lose.

If you are on a panel, watch out at all times. If someone else on the panel is answering or speaking, do not show disinterest, a smirk, or any expression you do not want the camera or audience to catch because they will, and again, you lose.

When you prepare answers ahead of time, build in at least three or four "gee-whizzes." Use colorful language and give important information to the public. That will be a big plus for your side. Give a fact that will make the audience say, "Gee whiz, I didn't know that." You and those three or four items will be the things they remember.

If you feel upset with yourself because you lacked the best answer, do not go back and try to redo it. You will usually make yourself look worse. The audience will let it go if you do not make a big deal out of it. Just continue on; keep creating that image for yourself of a benevolent, sincere, kind, and, above all, honest person.

If you get an interviewer who keeps stepping on your answer and doesn't let you finish, take charge. Seize the interview away from him by not answering his most recent question. Instead go back to the previous question by saying, "I would like to answer that question, but first let me complete my answer to your previous question."

What every interviewer wants is a good show, so don't give him short, three- or four- word, yes-or-no type answers. If you do, they are more likely to splice the tape together for your part, which may distort and hurt your image. They may even decide it was not a good interview and leave you out altogether.

Be careful with your business logic. Often business people come out with facts and logic. Remember, first you must go for those "gee-whizzes." Get that headliner out quick or they may cut you out before you get to your down-the-road punch line.

Remember not be grim all the time. Smile, be pleasant, and relax. Don't be too philosophical. Have a real natural sense of humor, but don't under any circumstances become a comedian. Give answers that are real. Don't defend things unnecessarily. Be real, be honest, be direct, and you win. Honesty about a problem becomes believable. Then, if you know concrete facts and figures, you become an immediate expert.

You can get excellent training in front of your own video camera at home or in the office. As you view yourself, ask, "How would the public perceive me?" Do you have a tic, a lot of "uhs," clearing of the throat, or any bothersome habits? Rehearse yourself over and over and over and over. Then you win for sure.

One of the cardinal rules of marketing yourself or your company through speaking is never to speak on a subject unless you know more about it than 75 percent of your audience. The way you test yourself is by asking whether you would feel completely comfortable to fielding any and all questions at the end of the speech. If you would be comfortable, then you probably are okay on the subject.

Since you know your subject, you do not have to read your speech, right? Right! That is a sin. Notes are okay to trigger your speech, but never read it. By the same token, do not memorize it. Memorization has gotten many into trouble. Remember the little seven-year-old who memorized his four lines for the Sunday school Christmas play, got up, and did the first two lines fine—then his mind went blank. Please believe me, it also happens to adults.

The best idea is to use three-by-five-inch index cards for a speech. Just use them as cue cards so you can keep all your points in line. This backs up your memory and eliminates the canned, reading method. After a few deliveries, you will be so proficient the audience will not know you are using anything. Then they will think you are brilliant, eloquent, superior, and believable.

If you want your audience to remember you and your speech, punch into it a short story for each point you want to make. I firmly believe Christ was the greatest teacher and speaker of all time. He used stories to illustrate each point he made, and we remember them two thousand years later. We were not even there to hear his speeches—we only read about them. Use short, pointed stories to plant your message firmly and people will enjoy listening to you.

If your personality will allow you, put drama and emotion into your speech. Make sure it is real. Phony tries will come across as phony. If this is against your nature, learn to do it by practicing whenever you can.

Above all, stay away from any off-color comments. Four-letter words and risqué jokes may be commonplace today, but not in quality speeches, interviews, or general conversation if you want to be respected.

When you are speaking, constantly look around into the faces of the audience. If spotlights prevent you from seeing their faces, just keep looking back and forth where those faces should be. This personalizes your talk, making it appear that you are speaking directly to them as individuals.

Remember always to use a microphone. Having to strain to hear is terrible. Many have small hearing problems anyhow. Acting like a big macho who doesn't need a microphone is for little poeple who don't know any better.

Don't be an ego tripper who uses buzzwords your industry understands but others in your audience may not. This is a simple matter of courtesy to your listeners. By the same token, don't oversimplify; it will seem like you are talking down to them.

31

The Other Departments

As You Need Them, Be Ready to Add Them

To open a shop is easy; the difficult thing is to keep it open. Chinese Proverb

You may do a tremendous sales volume, but if the other departments of the company do not function properly, it will eventually kill your sales. To go in and start functioning without guidelines for everyone wastes time and money and possibly places the entire business at risk. Yet many businesses have started in just that way. Many of those same companies are not in business today.

SETTING UP DEPARTMENTS

Departments need to be set up, on paper at least. Possibly you do not have a full-functioning need yet. Regardless, have a basis worked out in a manual for each prior to the full need arising. In addition to the ones we have discussed, a few of those departments might be:

1. Legal
2. Leasing
3. Supply
4. Shipping and receiving
5. Research and development
6. Construction
7. Warehousing
8. Personnel
9. Purchasing
10. Manufacturing
11. Mail handling
12. Printing

13. Data Processing
14. Maintenance
15. Security
16. Transportation
17. Customer service
18. Finance

19. Quality control
20. Production
21. Planning
22. Communications
23. Credit
24. Executive

You probably will not need nearly all of these in the beginning years. Time and growth may bring others into play.

When I say you should have a basis on paper, I mean at least have a manual completed for each department you will need in the next twelve months. Each department that has anything to do with franchisee operations should see that one of their manuals is given to each franchisee and/or manager as he or she progresses through the training class. Some manuals will be two inches thick; others may be only twelve pages. There will be several departments listed above that your company will not need at all. Putting methods, objectives, and directions on paper, in manuals, helps everyone to produce. you will also discover ideas as the formal manual process is put together.

Another important factor about putting things on paper is that it brings about uniformity for your people. They know exactly what "the plan" is and thus can comply. This may sound simple, but it is not an item that should be taken lightly. You may have the general direction and area of responsibility clearly depicted in your mind and think you have verbally conveyed the same to others. Believe me, you have not—it just doesn't happen that way.

People think they have the idea and they proceed. The process sometimes continues for years because the deviation is not one of great consequence. Thus, it goes unnoticed four or five steps up the line of management. Multiply that by dozens of little stops with different people and we have large time, money, or progress numbers to consider. I have a saying that fits here: "You're doing a great job—but you're doing it wrong."

32

Later On—Expansion

Twenty Items to Consider for Down the Road

The unconscious gradual downward slide is a human trait. The upward climb is a conscious decision.

To expand or not to expand, that is the question. Generally speaking, the answer is usually to expand. It is not that simple. First comes the marketplace; other things should follow. Some of them are:

1. Where exactly are your best markets?
2. Have you defined them specifically?
3. What are the time sequences for penetration?
4. How much will it cost?
5. What will be the mix of company-owned outlets to franchises?
6. How many locations will certain markets take?
7. Who will head up this expansion force?
8. How is the sales department geared for this?
9. Can you move key people to other areas?
10. Just what is your situation as to manpower now and in the future?
11. Will this have any negative effect on the existing operation or manpower?
12. Does your franchise agreement need changing now?
13. Will you sell licenses for area or sublicensing?

14. Can you realistically meet your time schedule, including legal filings in the numerous states?
15. Who will gear up the marketing departments?
16. Can marketing and media scheduling meet your time frames?
17. How much money will it take for all this and when will it happen?
18. Can existing suppliers service your expanded needs?
19. Will freight or other costs require new supplies closer to your new outlets?
20. Will the needs or taste of consumers in the new areas require changes in your present product, service, presentation methods, or any other part of your operation?

By now you are probably shaking your head and saying, Forget the whole thing. It may not be as bad as that. The important thing is to have a plan and know your limitations. Slower, well-planned growth, with limited capital, can also bring very satisfactory results. On the other hand, it can be devastating to see tremendous need in the marketplace, have a good track record, and launch into sales just because people will buy your franchise. You have to have the structure to back up your endeavors with finances, manpower, and all the rest. Just know for what size expansion you can successfully gear. That is the secret.

THINKING ABOUT SUBFRANCHISING

Often when a newer franchisor, who does not have unlimited funds, thinks of expansion, he thinks of area franchising or subfranchising. He thinks this is the least expensive way to proceed and still cover the map with outlets. Be careful with this philosophy. I have touched on some of the pitfalls earlier. Here are a few more.

Experience has proven that because of all the various undertakings and qualifications necessary, many new franchisors have been less than successful with area franchising. The number of potential franchisees who will make an investment of money and time large enough to develop an area is limited. There are surely a number of other money-making opportunities after that potential investor's capital. Area franchises generally permit subfranchising, which brings on control problems. Control problems usually have a tendency to increase your managing cost, and your problems compound. In addition, you usually get a smaller share of the royalty because it is shared with your area franchisor. This has an effect on your income stream.

If your area franchisee has subfranchising rights, there may be legal problems. Extreme care must be taken to avoid a chain or pyramid structure of sales. Generally, the laws prohibit sales of franchises by anyone below the area franchisor level. If the area franchisor is not selling subfranchises, but rather developing the entire territory himself, this may be a different situation. He probably is financially strong and is able to tier his management for success. You set up quotas on outlets and time periods, and actually deal with only one franchisee in this case. This has advantages and disadvantages. If the area franchisee gets large enough, the tail-wagging-the-dog problem often develops. He may start to change formats, policies, and almost anything else he decides. He has economic power and he may use it.

On the good side are all the obvious advantages, including the speedy growth of your system if you have chosen the area franchisee wisely. Your money, manpower, and desire will determine what route you take.

33

Considering International Markets

Knowing the Rules Is Number One for Success

Is it true that in Yourtown, USA, they have printed on the bottom of cola bottles, "Open other end"?

Certainly no one's town would need that printed on the bottom of a cola bottle! Don't be too sure—things are different in other countries. The difference might truly shock you after you have spent thousands of dollars there and there is still no sign of making your system work.

Let me tell you a true story. One of the large franchisors in this country decided to go to England. His company did some market studying, but not a total job. They thought since we both were English-speaking countries and England was our mother country, there would not be much difficulty; the differences would not be drastic. People were standing in line to buy their licenses, so they set about franchising and opening company-owned units. That was about the tenth mistake.

They fell on their faces or, I guess I should say, on their pocketbook. The beautiful, well-known, mighty, successful chain that was a household word here was like a fish out of water there. After losing a lot of money, they learned some lessons. They realized their errors and today, after heartache and correction, they are finally successful. If they had not had a lot of money behind them, the story might have ended differently, even for the home operation in the United States. The drain may have been too great to survive.

WHY YOU SHOULD NEVER ASSUME ANYTHING

First rule: Don't ever assume anything when it comes to foreign markets. I do not care if you spent the last sixteen vacations there. If you did not grow up and continue to live there, you don't know the customs and the way of life.

We have the reverse happening here in the United States today. A group from a foreign country has been buying outlets in a specific industry for several years now. They come here; buy; bring the brothers, sisters, and spouses; and attempt to continue the business. They are starting to resell outlets and take a loss. In fact, I recently bought an outlet from them. It was on its back and gasping for air. They just didn't understand our customs, business methods, laws, and so on. This, or any other, is only a land of opportunity if you know what you are doing. I have had the operation for eight months now and I am turning it around. Business is up about 24 percent so far. Sure, I have had to put money into redecorating and marketing, but that is what it takes. After all, what I am doing is the way we run a business here in the United States. It is our customs I am conscious of and accommodating.

Do not assume that foreign laws are even close to what you are used to here. I have run into everything from buying your way (graft) to being told you cannot do business there at all. Do not assume your business format or your operational policies will be accepted or even tolerated in a foreign country.

Services or products that you take for granted here may not be available at all there. Look again at the questions listed in the previous chapter. They are similar for a foreign market.

Taxes can be dramatically different elsewhere. Also, how Uncle Sam treats your profits is different from income earned here. You may need an "off-shore" operation or tiered levels through several countries.

The different in monetary rates and fluctuations can have a sizable effect on your business. So can tariffs in each direction. In what currency do you get your royalties? What trademark protection do you have? Language barriers can do strange things to business, and can even do strange things to a balance sheet.

There are some "dos" you should follow. Do your homework. Do it in every phase, in every operation, in every department. Success here does not guarantee even moderate success elsewhere. Consider being flexible with perhaps your entire system. Language, customs, climate, and almost any other differences may make it wise to modify designs, formula, colors, even name.

In the mid-seventies, I was doing a consulting job for a large Japanese company in connection with a motel franchise they were thinking of bringing to Japan. The word *motel* was part of the franchisor's name. My interpretor explained to me that the word *motel* could not be used there because that word meant house of ill repute or lovers' motel. If the franchisor went to Japan, they would have to modify their name.

HOW SMALL COMPANIES FRANCHISE

For a small- or moderate-size company (and often for a large franchisor) it is usually wise to deal with a local master franchisee for the country or region. This can be your biggest key success. He knows the customs and has the contacts to make your system work. In addition, if political trouble comes, a national has the best chance of continuing with your system. You would probably be out of luck otherwise.

Be sure and check out that master franchisee's potential. This is an extremely important choice which may determine success or failure for you in a whole country. Laws may work slowly or against you totally in many foreign countries. If you make a bad choice, you may be stuck with it.

Be prepared to spend more than you think you will. It always works that way. Transferring know-how, travel expenses, overcoming language problems, and dealing with misunderstandings are all expensive. Perhaps your time is the most expensive of all. You and your people will be spending it.

There is help you can obtain. The IFA has numerous associations from foreign countries which belong. We have helped set up several of these associations and through the IFA have brought about many contacts which have led to master franchises being put together. In addition, the IFA is a fostering member of what we call the World Council of Franchise Associations. One of its prime purposes is to organize and disseminate franchising information among the various member countries. This includes subject information relating to the franchising business in connection with financing, laws, statistics, types of barriers, trends, and other current positive aspects.

WHY COMPANIES ARE INTERESTED IN FOREIGN MARKETS

All of the caution in this chapter does not mean stop, nor does it mean that success in sizable measure is not there. The United States Department of Commerce sites several prime reasons why United States franchisors are interested in the growing foreign markets. It is because those markets are now showing:

1. Rising disposable income.
2. Improved conditions.
3. Improved transportation.
4. Growing demand for consumer goods and services.

SOME STATISTICS ON FOREIGN GROWTH

The growth of operational units in foreign countries far exceeds the growth rate at home. A large part of that can be credited to the fact that they are new ventures in a new market. Undoubtedly, as penetration of the marketplace continues in the future, the growth rate will moderate. The past decade tells the story: In 1971, there were 156 United States franchising companies operating 3,365 outlets in foreign countries. By the end of 1981, the numbers jumped to 288 companies with 21,416 units in the foreign markets—an 85 percent increase in franchisors and a sixfold increase in outlets.

Year	Number of Companies	Total Units	Percent Increase
1971	156	3,365	
1972	175	6,153	83%
1973	208	9,509	55%
1974	217	9,663	2%
1975	222	10,964	13%
1976	234	12,348	13%
1977	244	14,217	15%
1978	266	17,156	21%
1979	275	19,449	13%
1980	279	20,428	5%
1981	288	21,416	5%
1982	295	23,524	9%
1983	305	25,682	8%

Surveys reveal that of the 305 companies doing business overseas in 1983, 286 sell their outlets to franchisees either directly or through a master licensee who is developing the country or area. Forty-one operated joint ventures; only thirty-three had some company-operated units.

Of those 305 companies, twenty-three derived 10 percent or more of their income from foreign operations; twenty firms received 5–9 percent, ninety-four received 1–4 percent, and 164 received less than 1 percent.

Naturally, Canada is the leading marketplace for United States franchisors, with 30 percent of the foreign franchised outlets there in 1982. There are 217 franchisors with 7,765 units in Canada. Of those, 1,306 are in nonfood retailing, 1,539 are in restaurant operations, and 1,003 are in business aids and services.

Japan is the second largest market with 5,079 outlets, of which 69 percent are food related, such as fast food restaurants, ice cream stores, doughnut shops, and convenience stores.

The United Kingdom is third with 2,229 outlets. The entire continental European market only has a total of 4,370. The basic geographic foreign markets as of 1983 are distributed as follows:

Geographic Area	Number of Units
Canada	7,765
Japan	5,079
Continental Europe	4,370
United Kingdom	2,229
Australia	2,137
Asia	1,033
Caribbean	713
Africa	595
Mexico	496
South America	467
New Zealand	380
Near East	262
Central America	156

Since many countries are now awakening to the desirability of encouraging franchising, the opportunities look better. A recent survey revealed forty-four additional franchisors wanted to expand into foreign markets in the near future. A good portion of these are fast food companies. If you decide to go, I hope your grass is green on the other side of the fence—the kind of green that has "In God We Trust" printed on it.

FOREIGN FRANCHISE ASSOCIATIONS

The following are the foreign associations that are affiliated with the IFA at this time:

Australia—Franchisors Association of Australia

Brussels—Belgian Franchising Association

Canada-Association of Canadian Franchisors

Denmark—Danish Franchisor Association

England—British Franchise Association

—European Franchise Federation

France—French Franchise Association

Ireland—Irish Franchise Association

Italy—Italian Franchise Association

Japan—Japan Franchise Association

Netherlands—Dutch Franchise Association

Sweden—Swedish Franchise Association

South Africa—South African Franchise Association

Switzerland—Swiss Franchise Association

34

The Importance of and How to Work With Legislators

Getting and Giving Legislative Assistance

Left to themselves, things go from bad to worse.   Murphy's First Law

There is a saying you may possibly may have seen many times, "Due to mass apathy, tomorrow will be cancelled." There seems to be a general feeling of "I'm just one person. What can I do about it?" That kind of thinking is where trouble starts. Much can be accomplished by one person.

A few years ago, I was talking to some legislators in Washington about this very subject of what one person can do. One of the Congressmen commented, "If I get thirty letters on one subject, I know it is important and I had better look into it." The other legislators standing around seemed to agree with him. Over the years, as I have worked with various legislators at the state and federal level, I have found that things work when people do. The main problem is educating the congressmen and senators. There is so much going on, with so much information trying to make its way through their offices, it is literally impossible for them to absorb it all. The letters, which are quite often handled by aides, and/or the personal contacts with the aides and the representatives are the things that pay off. Changes do come about if you make the effort.

SETTING UP ONE PERSON FOR THE JOB

Let's look at some ideas concerning how your company can have an effective program encompassing government relations. I think one of the most important points is to designate one particular employee to act as the person in charge of governmental affairs. This may be just a small portion of his job description, but include it in that description. At least someone is doing something. There is another saying, "Everyone's responsibility is no one's responsibility. This is just what happens if you don't designate one specific person to handle governmental affairs.

That person's duties may include some of the following:

1. He or she would handle all the mail concerning governmental regulations or proposed or existing legislation. After all, someone has to inform your people of things that have already taken place.
2. That same person would serve as a contact for such organizations as your particular industry association and the IFA, since both deal a lot in the area of governmmental action programs.
3. This person would, as time permits, endeavor to get to know the legislators and government officials and perhaps develop some type of rapport which would be beneficial in time of need. You may even want to create a political action committee in order to collect moneys to be used for the benefit of potential legislators who are sympathetic to your ideas.
4. The employee designated would be the one to communicate with the legislators by visit, telegram, or in writing.

It is very, very important that someone also be responsible for follow-up communications when contacts come back from the legislator's office. If you want to know more about how one can participate and be active in this area, you might want to contact the Chamber of Commerce of the United States, Legislative Affairs Department, 1615 H Street NW, Washington, DC 20062. They have good information available for just this type of situation.

Be careful how you use corporate funds for political purposes, especially in federal elections. Some states will allow you to contribute both financial and in-kind services toward state and local elections. You should consult legal counsel to be sure of your particular state's statutes. You may want to grant leaves of absence to employees so they may work on behalf of a candidate or party; however, you must be cautious to be sure it is without pay in certain types of elections. Otherwise, that could be considered a contribution. There are numerous types of political education programs which can be put on for your employees; you can also invite candidates on a bipartisan basis to come and address some of your meetings. You may want to explain the various issues to your employees, suppliers, and perhaps customers, so they can get in on the contacting of legislators.

SOME USEFUL COMMUNICATIONS TOOLS

I guess if I had to rate the types of communications with legislators, I would have to say the personal letter is number one. Let me emphasize the word *personal*. A congressman or any of his staff can clearly detect a movement that is bringing in several letters with similar wording. Likewise, form letters go way down on the list of importance. One concise, well-thought-out, intelligent personal letter probably means more than a thousand names on a petition or form letter.

I do not want to underemphasize volume in relation to mail. Volume is very important. If you could get fifteen of your employees using their home addresses to write personal letters, not on any corporate stationary, you would have a sizable campaign started. If they know these thaings affect their jobs and business, there is a good chance they would be willing to write. My experience has been that employees feel important when you consult them and ask for assistance. They are honored to help. This is, of course, if they agree with your philosophy in connection with the particular problem.

On an average, a representative at the federal level receives about 450 to 475 letters per week, while a senator generally receives from 1,000 to 2,000, depending on the amount of interest in the specific bills up at that time. Naturally, most of your communications should go to your particular legislators. If you are a franchisor with operations in various states, you can quickly enlist the assistance of your franchisees and their employees in those states to contact their particular legislators. A tremendous ground swell of writing can be accomplished through your network.

The availability and effectiveness of a network is often measured by the speed with which it can act. If you get a word that a certain bill is going to be reported favorably out of subcommittee within the next three days, you don't have time to organize your network and instruct them how to go about wiring a letter. You need your network now, with particular people designated in franchisee operations to handle this type of thing when speed is necessary. It can all happen very quickly.

The effect your network can have is almost unbelievable. I've seen it work many, many times and bring satisfactory results. I am not suggesting by any means that you should have your network set up to feather your own nest undeservingly. That is not the way the free enterprise system works. We have far too many people arguing for particular segments of our population now. It is all right to educate legislators so proper decisions can be made. It is not all right to have protective legislation passed merely to protect oneself at the expense of everyone else.

WHO TO WRITE TO AND WHAT TO WRITE

When you are writing, be sure the exact name and address you are writing to are on the letter and not just on the envelope. Envelopes quite often get destroyed when they are opened. The letters will then go on to the proper desk. Always write on personal stationery or corporate letterhead. By the way, don't forget the corporate citizen is just that—a citizen—in the eyes of our legislators. I guess if I had to choose for importance in the legislator's eyes, I would have to say the handwritten letter that is neatly done carries more weight than anything else. When you are addressing the legislation, I would suggest it be as follows:

For the Senate:

Honorable John Doe
United States Senate
Washington, DC 20510

Dear Senator Doe:

For the House of Representatives:

Honorable John Doe
House of Representatives
Washington, DC 20515

Dear Congressman Doe:

In writing the letter, you should start off by identifying yourself as a constituent, whether it be corporate or personal. The fact that you did not vote for the man is not important at this point. He is your elected official. If for some reason you write to a legislator who is not a direct representative of yours, you should also send a copy of the letter to your congressman and ask him to contact the other legislator on your behalf. Next, state your topic clearly and make reference to the bill by title and number if it has already been introduced.

State specifically the exact impact the legislation will have on you, your business or community. Use examples and numbers if you can put them together. Above all, be sure your information is correct; put it in your own words. Don't copy it down from someplace else.

Ask your legislator for a specific action. Ask him to vote for it or against it. Ask him to have it delayed. Ask him to give you information or whatever the situation might be. But ask specifically for an exact action. If the situation warrants, ask for his position on the particular issue.

Be sure to keep letters short. Have your mailing timed so it arrives in Washington on Tuesday, Wednesday, or Thursday. Stay away from Monday and Friday arrival dates. Do not ask for the impossible; be reasonable with your request. Never threaten the legislator; be firm, polite, and to the point. If he should support your position, be sure to thank him.

Many people forget to do this. If he does not vote the way you would like him to, be sure to let him know you are aware of how he voted and that you disagree. On extremely important issues, be sure you follow up with a telephone call to his office and an appointment if possible.

HOW AND WHEN TO USE THE TELEGRAM, MAILGRAM, AND TELEPHONE

If response time is especially critical, use a telegram or mailgram. The same things apply to telegrams as to letters. However, because of their expense, I am sure you will want to keep them much simpler and more to the point. The mailgram is relatively inexpensive, and Western Union guarantees next-day deliver in the contiguous forty-eight states. Western Union also charges a lesser rate for mailgrams going to Congress and to the President than it does for regular telegrams or mailgrams.

If you know the congressman or senator personally, a telephone call is usually very, very powerful. Even if you don't know him or her you can usually get through if it is a critical issue and you are determined. This emphasizes the point of how important it is to know these legislators prior to something critical coming up. If you should make contact by telephone, like a good scout, be prepared. Know what the various issues are, be familiar with the various provisions, have a little outline to go by so you can be sure to touch all points, and, if time permits, try to precede your telephone call with a letter which includes the statement that you will be calling on such and such a day. Outline the points in the letter so it will be in front of him or her and you won't have to go over the whole thing again by telephone. If there is difficulty in making contact, talk with one of the staff members and offer to adjust your schedule so you can be near a specific telephone during a certain period of time when he or she can call you back.

Finally, don't abuse the telephone or the personal meeting privilege. If the matter isn't critical, allow yourself time and send a letter. If you should need to telephone to get through to members of Congress, you can call (202) 224-3121. Just ask for the particular senator or representative you want by name and state.

If you should want to make an appointment to see the congressman, whether it be at his or her office in Washington or back in the district, get hold of either office, depending on where you want the appointment to take place. Ask for the appointment secretary, tell that person what you want to talk about, the particular legislation you are interested in, and when you would like to see the congressman. When you go to see him or her, follow the same rules as apply to a telephone call. Be a good scout—be prepared, be exact, and don't waste time. State your position, thank the representative, and leave.

Remember that saying, "For the want of a nail...." You, too, can be like the little Dutch boy who placed his finger in the hole in the dyke and saved the nation.

35

The Qualities of a Gentle Tiger

How to Pick Successful People

The tiger and the calf may lie down together, but the calf won't get much sleep.

With the various evolutions through which society has passed in the last four or five decades, can a company president still find a tiger for his team? The answer is yes. And to prove it, I hired one!

The charging tigers who still have the gentle yet wise techniques of a kitten are still out there...and doing well. In years gone by, we may have looked for a tough tiger or two. Today we must have a gentle tiger, still a tiger in every way, but with understanding and compassion to go along with all the fighting characteristics. He or she knows how to lead, produce, create, and evaluate.

I guess the next question should be, Is there still a need for these gentle tigers? Definitely yes! As long as there is a free enterprise capitalistic system of economics, there will always be a need for people who can compete well in a given environment.

Following the economic slowdown of the 1973–76 period, our country began moving toward conservatism. This was especially true in financial areas. With this feeling of "move slowly and with caution," some may have thought the tiger was no longer needed. This is not the case at all. The quick-shooting fast dealer who made headlines for himself during the twenties or the merger-merger-merger sixties may not appear the same. In fact, he or she probably is not the same. The new generation has developed more of a professional person who knows about the X and Y

186

management philosophies and who has acquired the new Z methods with polish.

This person has advanced in skill and mellowed in technique. His or her predecessor would not even recognize him or her. The fast-dealing, tough, curt managerial policies are now balanced with other qualities of a good professional manager of people. He or she is highly tuned to ROI (return on investment), ROE (return on equity), ROA (return on assets), and other such requirements. No matter what one calls it, it all amounts to what is on the bottom line.

WHAT ARE THE DESIRED EXECUTIVE QUALIFICATIONS?

What goes into making a Gentle Tiger? This may be very good to know because you might need one someday...or you may already have one. Certainly if you have or if you acquire a Gentle Tiger, you need to know what makes this person tick and how to feed him.

A Gentle Tiger makes decisions. This is a big reason he is in demand today. He faces challenges head-on. He is not afraid to take that fabled bull by the horns and make a decision. He knows how to gather facts quickly, utilize the knowledge and assistance of subordinates, and above all, balance that mental scale between logic, emotion, social responsibility, and profits. It takes a tiger for job requirements like these.

He is not wishy-washy, but decisive. The people who have to make decisions all the time, the people who are good at it, are positive thinkers, according to a recent study of top corporate executive and independent business entrepreneurs undertaken at the University of Michigan School of Business Administration. When faced with new products and new ideas, the good decision makers view them in terms of the opportunity or profit. The executive who constantly shoots down new ideas may be too negative to be effective.

Decision making is a learned process of examining and weighing the available choices and comparing the probable success of each. Ideally, learning to make decisions should start in early childhood; some youngsters are never given the opportunity.

What separates the good decision makers from the poor ones? They are able to reduce complex situations to their essentials, getting right to the core of the problem, and see their way directly to what seems the obvious course of action. The answers are easy once you have determined the questions. Success in decision making leads to further success. People who have real confidence in their ability to make good decisions are also self-reliant and well balanced, according to studies at the University of California.

Since our Gentle Tiger does not want to commit business suicide, he must also be temperate. To ignore intelligent advice—and not asking for it is the same as ignoring it—means there is the possibility of great calculated risk. He gathers advice and tempers his personal feelings and desires in the face of reason. He establishes good backup plans just in case.

With the proliferation of information, the strides of motivational techniques, and the pace of consumer demand for change, a Gentle Tiger has learned to rely on his people. Knowing this, he has chosen them with all the skill of a surgeon. He has learned to evaluate and truly communicate with them. He keeps them aware of their good and bad performance on a daily basis. While he may still use the six-month or yearly personnel evaluation system for salary and billet purposes, he actually evaluates his people moment to moment as the tasks are performed. People learn to trust and thus like this very much. In addition, his personnel respect him because it is comfortable to always know where one stands with the boss. Moment-to-moment evaluation produces this respect.

A Gentle Tiger has trained himself to be an intuitive creative thinker. This is not a skill most people possess. Everyone would like to believe he is a creative thinker, but to be an intuitive creative thinker is something else. Not only does the Gentle Tiger's mind instantly see the unique and different, but he can expeditiously measure its possibility for success. He is sensitive to his customers, their desires, and the relativity of these to the probability of a successful conclusion.

The Gentle Tiger has a clear division in his mind between business and personal goals. Without this ability, he may be impeding his business potential. A person may have a very strong desire to achieve, but in what direction can this be realized? To some achievers, that need may be satisfied by off-the-job activities—by being president of the yacht club, chairman of the United Fund, or a behind-the-scenes political leader. If that is the case, his need to achieve may be satisfied off the job. On the job, he may be a regular fellow instead of a tiger.

Calculated risks are another area where the Gentle Tiger seems to do well. To outsiders, it might appear that he takes big chances, but to himself that is not the case at all. What outsiders are not aware of is that our Gentle Tiger has analyzed the information available from his trusted people, the independent outside sources, and his knowledge of business in general to form a basis of reasonableness. The decision was then removed from high risk to logical conclusion. Today, million-dollar decisions in the regulated, competitive, fast-reacting marketplace need more than the "old gut reaction." If the risk situation does come along, our Tiger will use everything possible to cover all the bases. If that still fails, he will quickly salvage and move on. He will not hang onto a bad situation and hope. He takes his losses and learns.

Status quo is great for the recipe for Mom's homemade rolls, but not for the Gentle Tiger. He relishes progress, and that usually means change. His people understand he is always open, really open, to suggestion and likes to see creative things come to pass. Thus, his people are constantly thinking of how to do it better, faster, in a less costly way, and with a stylish flair. This method assists in keeping the flame of personal-achievement satisfaction burning in everyone around our Tiger.

Our Gentle Tiger allows each person to be a self-motivator by idea flowup through the corporate structure. Everyone likes to be an entrepreneur. Being open enough to reject status quo brings about what I refer to as *fluid drive*. This is a drive that is smooth yet powerful. It races toward self-actualization. Mankind has certain basic psychological needs. There are strong desires to have those needs fulfilled. Our most basic needs are to belong to a group, for clothing, shelter, sexual gratification, and so on. Generally, those desires do not play as dominant a role in motivation as most still think, because in the present-day United States they are basically satisfied. A want that is satisfied is no longer a want. The dominant need which seems to be unfulfilled is that of personal ego reward. Every employee is certainly not a corporate ladder climber. Many may feel personal achievement while continuing on the same job. Our Tiger has the ability to allow this. In fact, he encourages it.

The Gentle Tiger has another extremely valuable talent. He has common sense. This is not necessarily extracted from books, for we all know people with several college degrees who do not have common sense. When one is gathering information toward a decision, this element of realism, of common sense, is of vital importance. Risk potentials often call for commonsense interpretation to select the best option. This commonsense factor is a must for every leader. Subordinates may not know exactly what is right in many cases; however, they recognize quickly the elements of realistic, commonsense evaluation.

Making a bad decision is normal, providing it does not happen too often. With the power to decide goes the right to either success or failure. We must understand and expect wrong decisions occasionally. If you make no decisions for yourself, but always operate under your boss's decisions, only then can you avoid making mistakes. Likewise, you are just a puppet. Our Gentle Tiger is aware that he will occasionally make a bad decision.

His good business and psychological understandings allow him to accept it, learn, and continue to strive. If he should make a bad decision, he will react and recuperate, causing as little damage as possible.

The Gentle Tiger has the attitude of a winner. You can feel it when you are with him, yet he does not intimidate you. Likewise, our Tiger is not intimidated by regulations, rules, or those in high stations—respectful, perhaps, but not intimidated. He accepts the idea that rules are negotiable. He uses the reasonableness of common sense, experiences of the past (and/or the present), and the advantages of intuitive creativity, all of which may bring about a change in the rules. The Tiger's attitude is unquestionably a positive one. He combines the essence of power with intelligent compassion. To think power is to have power.

Reading through the book *Future Shock*, one realizes the need for a faster reaction time. A Gentle Tiger has just that, fast reaction time, a necessity in today's business world. The warning signals come on us faster than before. He must respond quickly and with less business freedom than our forefathers. He is capable of this because he possesses qualities necessary to become a Gentle Tiger.

As you can quickly observe, today's manager must have very broad managerial skills, expertise, and discipline; be highly visible to his employees; and above all, have the ability to get the best out of his people. There are no rewards for efforts; rewards are granted for results.

By the way, are *you* a Gentle Tiger?

36

The Philosophy of Working with People

Do These Things and You Will Succeed

In any organization there is always one person who knows what is going on. This person must be fired.

For the insecure executive, department head, or line sergeant, that philosophy is often the safest. For an individual who is secure in his own self-worth, nothing could be further from the truth. Yet in any company there may be insecure people who often consciously impede the company's progress, their own, and the progress of those around and especially under them. Because they have been with the company for a while or have a basic handle on the portion of their job which says "Put the round peg in the round hole," many bosses are reluctant or don't think they have the time to make a change. If you are that type of boss, let me assure you it is costing you tenfold that price to keep them. It costs in time, with indirect problems that develop. It costs in other employees, who quit. It costs in good employees who have real potential who are fired or forced gradually (often in an unseen way) to resign.

Often these insecure people will have moved up to a position of authority. Sometimes that makes the correction harder—perhaps impossible. I once had a problem like that. When it finally dawned on me what (who) the problem was, he was a vice president. We sat down and talked. It took a few hours, but we arrived at a point of understanding. He recognized the problem, and together we set a time limit. We would discuss it monthly with a six-month maximum for change or resignation. Together, we concluded it probably would take psychological help to solve the situation. One month, two months, three months went by with a like number of meetings on the subject. He concluded that he had these personality reaction traits deeply entrenched. "I guess if I wanted to change, I would. I just don't think I want to badly enough." That was his conclusion. He resigned, and the department started taking sizable steps forward with its good, now-growing, progressive people. Cooperation improved between that department and others. The progress was all positive.

MY TWENTY-FIRST CENTURY
MANAGEMENT TECHNIQUES

Most of us have studied X- and Y-type management principles in college or at various seminars. Recently, a professor at Harvard wrote a book about a Japanese style of management he calls Z-type management. It is basically what I have been teaching in seminars and consulting on for several years. Believing it to be the new wave of the future, I had been calling my theory "Twenty-First Century Management Techniques." No matter what you call it, the theory works. It produces greater results, more quickly, and with more human gratification than anything I have ever seen in any type of organization. Here is what Twenty-First Century Management Techniques are all about.

As a student of human behavior, I had read many of the great psychologists and psychiatrists from Freud to the modern day, including Abraham Maslow. In several of Maslow's works he dissected what he called the hierarchy of needs, the human need for food, clothing, shelter, air, to belong to a group, sexual gratification, and so on. There was one he discussed at great length, the ego need. As he described his philosophies, he stated how these basic needs were generally all satisfied to some extent in our American culture except this ego need. It was not fulfilled for many either in personal life and/or in the business world. Yet that world is where a great part of the fulfillment is sought.

As I pondered this, I was led to more of an open-door type of policy. I endeavored to teach my department heads to listen to their people more. This met with some success, but was nowhere near what was to come later.

That success began to unfold in 1974 when I was doing consulting work in connection with a large conglomerate firm in Japan. During my work there, I had to tour all four of the main islands. One day, my interpreter told me he and the chauffeur had to be back in the home office in two days for a meeting. Realizing we were some distance away, on another island, I asked what was going on. He explained that the company was considering some new ideas and they had to be at the meetings to make suggestions. I questioned him about the chauffeur attending. He said everyone in the company (and they employed thousands) would be needed for their ideas on the project.

They allowed me to attend, and there I saw real brainstorming. I also saw the high value management placed upon everyone's comments. During the rest of my trip, I pondered what I had seen. It had appeared somewhat similar to what I did back home. I did not realize at the time that it was vastly different.

The big difference was that here I held the open sessions with my executive officers and department heads. They in turn supposedly held brainstorming sessions with their people on the same subjects, then they fed information back up to the executive level. Communications, with various people handling the meetings and everyone's perceptions of what then happened to their ideas, made up part of the big difference. That's a big problem in the business world. Communications, and how people understood or misunderstood, was at the forefront once again. I still did not have it all tied together in my mind.

One day, the Securities Exchange Commission called. They wanted the latest copy of our corporate organizational chart. You know, the one with all the little boxes showing the president on top, with lines going down to the vice presidents and others until it gets to the managers, secretaries, and clerks on the lower position. I turned to the credenza in back of me and pulled the chart out of the drawer. It came out upside down. Then the light clicked on. That was it—Maslow's better feed-up and feed-down information, production, and all the rest. It began to come together.

PUTTING THE CASH REGISTER RINGERS ON TOP

The people on the bottom of the organizational chart are the ones on the firing line every day. They are where the customers are, they are where the sales are, where the cash register rings, where the end results come about. They are the ones who take in all the money. The executives decree how to spend it and rarely have much contact with the end user. Those on the bottom of that chart know more about the problems, too.

In Japan, I had seen everyone, from bottom to top, get their ideas in. Many of those on the daily firing line had good ideas for correcting problems and designing new methods. After all, who would know more about the problems of running the dishwasher in a restaurant than the busboy, who runs one. He knows that the nozzles on the left side keep stopping up or has an idea to do a better job by changing the timer ninety seconds on the second cycle. When you add up all the little things, you have success.

Then Maslow's theory tied in. The Japanese had everybody's brains involved. More brains means better products, more possible problems solved before they happen, and all the other obvious benefits. After taking everyone's ideas, management sifted out the best ones and then held another meeting on those thoughts. The "widget" is beginning to take shape now. They go through more refining steps, then managment says "*You* had a great idea, let's do it!" Now everyone perceives it as their idea (parts of which really are). They go to work. People like to see their ideas succeed, so they put forth their best efforts to accomplish just that. Maslow's ego rewards take hold and quality production runs very high. No one wants to let their ideas down. They feel good about achieving. Egos are rewarded. I call it psychic income.

We had used brainstorming. What was the difference? One was that most CEOs say they have an open-door policy, but they do not follow that principle psychologically. It is only partially true or just sounds good. The CEO or department head feels important by saying he is open to that type of management, but it takes thorough training for top management before they can get the hang of this. Few companies actually can develop this for maximum benefit without help. It also takes training of the employees before true sharing will occur. In many cases, the employees also believe they have participative management practices in their company; usually they do not.

THE CONCRETE RESULTS

After training our employees and top management (brainwashing is also a good word), the results were tremendous. Here is one example.

By the latter part of 1974, it was obvious that the energy crisis, inflation, skyrocketing costs, and lack of mortgage money were here to stay for a while. Until that point we had done nothing except build new motels. Mortgage money had not been available for some months. How do we expand in the budget motel field when mortgage money is nonexistent and doesn't look good for the future? By now our people were familiar with my Twenty-First Century Management Techniques or upside-down management, as some called it. When we wanted ideas about anything of any consequence we called a meeting of all employees. I had a large, six-foot bulletin board on wheels, nicknamed the "people board." We would call the meeting, post the questions on the board, and everyone would suggest their ideas. Each one was put on the board. There are five rules for using the people board: One, the more ideas the better. Two, you can piggyback on another's idea. Three, no idea is silly or too far in left field to be put up. Four, every idea must be expressed in a positive fashion. Five, after all ideas are on the board, try brainstorming the question or idea in the five senses: sight, sound, touch, smell, and taste. There again, you may not think your question or idea relates to one or possibly any of the senses, but you will be surprised what people think of. That will trigger someone else's thoughts on something, and a whole new train of thought will develop.

This particular day, we announced on the public address system that there would be a general meeting at 4 P.M. At that hour, everyone was there, eager to begin. The problem was, "How do we expand when we cannot get mortgage money?" During the course of the hour a secretary said, "Why don't we convert motels that are already built. They are already financed." The operations department chimed in, "We have thought of that before, but we doubt we can make them work. After all, a lot of these properties have swimming pools, restaurants, large lobbies, meeting rooms, and lounges. All of that has to be paid for and maintained through a higher rate on the motel rooms. Since we are in the budget business, I doubt we could make a pofit with our type of lower rates."

Until then we had built only guest rooms with a small lobby for guest registration. We had no pools, restaurants, or other extras. About that time, someone from marketing said, "How do we know our operational systems and marketplace appeal aren't strong enough to make it work?" This was batted around very positively for a while. It was now 5 P.M., time for the office to close, but people wanted to keep going with the ideas. They enjoyed being a part of formulating ideas and policy (management, if you will). Maslow's ego needs were being fed honestly. We took a five-minute break so people who wanted to could leave or get on the telephone to call babysitters, spouses, and so on to tell them they would be working late. Almost everyone stayed. Now back to the people board.

We finally closed up the session about six o'clock with a board full of ideas, some strange, some elementary, all valuable. Senior management took the board and over the next week sifted out the possible ideas. Some were just not practical, possible, or probable. Some triggered and brought about minor changes in policies and departments which were actually unrelated to the original problem posed. One area seemed to survive: Convert already-financed and built properties.

The following week we had another general meeting. The question this time was, "If conversion might work, how should we go about testing it?" Again, ideas came forth for the board. The franchise sales department volunteered to get a franchisee guinea pig for the test. Other departments had ideas. Everybody agreed that each department should put together a plan and be ready to move on the test case as soon as a volunteer franchisee was located.

Within ninety days the sales department had a volunteer; things started to move fast. Enthusiasm was running high. It was a tremendous success! We didn't know our operational methods were so strong. Costs were slashed in almost every area of that franchisee's operation. Occupancy went up. Within twelve months, he called and asked us to convert the other motel he owned to an Econo Lodge, which we did. Not so long ago he found some mortgage money, and now he has three motels in our system, with the fourth under construction.

Today, this conversion program is a division of our company and has become the fastest-growing segment we have. We kept a log on that first test case, which was fifty miles from the home office. It really could not have gone any other way. In looking over the log later, the entries revealed Abraham Maslow's thoughts about to what length people will go to receive ego reward, psychic income. There were entries like this:

Sunday, April 14: Took the family and rode up to see the motel. My husband took the kids to the park while I spent 2½ hours with the manager. (Signed), Marketing Director

Saturday, April 20: My wife and I were returning from niece's wedding in Richmond so we took a little detour by the motel. Wife took family to dinner while I worked with assistant manager and head housekeeper for two hours. (Signed), Operations Director

On their own time as well as during regular working hours, everybody made *their* idea work. With everyone putting their brains, efforts, and hearts behind the project, there was no way it could fail. It was a 100 percent effdort.

Some investigative institutions have estimated that under the normal hierarchy of corporate business structure, about 72 percent effort is put behind orders that management hands down. That certainly will not come out ahead of a 100 percent effort. Rather than orders going down, through upside-down managmenet the ideas flow *up* from the ranks. Management merely sifts through the ideas, takes the good one, and goes back and says, "That is a good idea *you* have, let's do it."

WHAT'S BETTER THAN 100 PERCENT RESULTS

This method has other benefits. As people receive psychic rewards (income), they feel more a part of the company. Absenteeism goes down. Employee turnover is less. People expand themselves in their jobs. They take on more responsibility. Their capabilities grow. Creative innovations flourish.

As people take more responsibilities on their shoulders, management is freed to have more time to manage, to plan, to dream, to think—all of which top executives should be doing anyway rather than fighting the day-to-day problems. Your organization expands and makes more money. As you do that, you can afford to give raises and benefits to those hard-working employees. That makes the cycle roll faster, and the benefits occur faster and go further.

Eighteen months after starting this program, we were handling 33 percent more properties with a ratio of 30 percent less people than before. As one would retire, move away, get pregnant, or whatever, others would come into my office and volunteer to take on the departing employee's duties. They wanted the additional challenge. They did the job and loved every minute of it.

Call it Z management, Twenty-First Century Management Techniques, upside-down management, or whatever you like, it is a wonderful way to run a railroad.

HOW TO STEM EMPLOYEE BURNOUT

Since this chapter is on working with people, let me touch on the same subject from a different aspect. There may be people in your organization who seem to have lost their zip. Maybe the old enthusiasm is not like it was two years ago. Perhaps they have become more negative in their thinking. Or maybe they just seem to be putting in time. I dare say every organization of any size probably has someone who fits one of these descriptions.

There does not seem to be any set pattern. They come in all sizes, can be found in any department and in any age group. It does not necessarily apply only to males; it is a disease that attacks females as well. We refer to this disease as *burnout*.

Management must remember to be aware of this problem and then be wise enough to solve it for the benefit of all. While everyone is susceptible to burnout, it does not have to be a terminal disease. Left alone, it often will be terminal.

Burnout does not apply only to the business environment. Many marriages are often referred to as having lost their spark. In today's world they often end up in divorce. Sometimes the parties are able to recognize and take the proper medicine to overcome the disease. For some, there is no medicine made that will cure them. No matter what the situation, for most of us it is a long-term and ongoing problem in connection with attitude and performance. Of course, all of us have our ups and downs, but they are mostly short-lived. But for those who get into an attitude rut, it usually requires some type of management surgery to assist the person in getting well.

Probably the best way to deal with burnout is to prevent it from happening in the first place. The most effective way I have ever seen is to allow or create situations whereby individual job enrichment is provided. An astute manager who is aware of the situation will learn to assess and allow each employee within his domain to know exactly where they stand at all times. He will learn to recognize individuals for the job they do on an almost daily basis. He will be appreciative of their inventiveness and constantly warmed by their desire to know more. He allows them—in fact, encourages them—to make wider decisions and new decisions within their capabilities. He will learn to encourage and expect creativeness within their job assignments. The manager will encourage his people to broaden their responsibilities.

The executive who knows his people shows sincere concern for what is happening to them and will go a long way in keeping the flames alive and burning well. He will be cognizant of their personal needs and help them consistently organize well-defined higher goals.

HOW TO DEAL WITH DIFFERENT IDEAS

All of this sounds like a lot of very basic words, and I guess they really are. However, if an executive is truly concerned and thinks he understands exactly how his people feel, try this little experiment. Let us assume the various jobs in your organization have well-defined descriptions. For the moment, do not look at those descriptions. Pick out a particular employee who you think may have lost some of his spark. Sit down at your desk and try to write out exactly what you think his job description is. After you complete this, call him in and ask him to tell you verbally what he thinks his job is. As he discusses this with you, write down what he is saying. Later, compare that to what you thought his job was and the actual job description as it is written in the file. You will find there are things left out, there are things he has not thought about, and probably you will find that you had a somewhat different opinion.

Now go back to those three job descriptions you have before you. Do they sound exciting? Is there real room for group and personal improvement? Or is it sort of dry? Does it have excitement by allowing for creativity and expansion, or is it something like pouring water on a fire? Maybe this is exactly what has caused his burnout.

In looking at the job descriptions, or thinking about your leadership with your people, how much real creativity is allowed? How much decision-making room is there for that individual? How much job expansion is really encouraged? We all realize that people's talents, skills, and interests change. Has the job changed accordingly, or has it expanded beyond the employee's current abilities? It could be a Peter Principle situation.

There are real opportunities that lie in the areas of education and moving up. When someone is encouraged to learn something new—when he can see a real reason for self-expansion—the flame will usually start to burn again. Brainstorming with others about solutions to real problems usually brings about different experiences with creative ideas. I am sure you can see here how Z management fits right in.

Sometimes the real executive is so busy with his day-to-day activities that he does not have a chance to get close to some of his people. Perhaps he really does not know where the burnouts have occurred. How about trying to get in touch with the grapevine? Every office has one, and it can often prove very valuable. Most people who suffer from burnout condition begin to radiate it. It is picked up by others and sometimes talked about quite openly. Most people do not like that kind of condition; they do not want that black cloud hanging over their heads. Perhaps it is indirect, perhaps it is subconscious and they really do not know what is going on. But there are usually telltale signs, and a sharp senior executive should not let them pass.

If the senior executive has a truly honest and open atmosphere between himself and his subordinates, the employee will usually communicate—that is, providing the executive makes the opportunity for him to do so. He may have to start talking about the employee's family, health, or personal life in some form. This will usually bring about an opening, since most stresses complicate all facets of one's life.

HOW TO RECOGNIZE WHAT IS NOT SAID

One of the first steps, then, is to recognize—recognize and, together with the individual, investigate the burnout. Endeavor to pinpoint what is true and what is not. How real is it, and how deep does it go? Quite often in our lives the thing we view as cause is not cause at all, but merely effect. Honest examination may reveal something entirely different from what is on the surface. Sometimes the person is underutilized in a particular job classification; this may be the cause that manifests itself in various ways. Sometimes it may be caused by other individuals in the organization. All of this must be pinned down exactly.

One of the greatest helps I have found is to write down facts when certain situations present themselves. As I sit down and begin to write, often things will materialize that were not in the forefront of my initial conscious efforts. Sometimes I wind up going back and changing things around after I have reached the end. As I have proceeded through the writing, patterns develop that actually bring about obvious firsthand assumptions.

Once you have pinned down what you think is the cause, then it becomes time to face it openly with the individual. As mentioned before, it is hoped that you have an honest and trusting relationship with the individual. Otherwise, an open discussion will be very difficult. Presuming you do have the desired relationship, then honesty and frankness can usually rule out the unreal situations. People certainly do not want to make problems for themselves. So, in the proper atmosphere of openness, most people generally are willing to try to discuss and find a solution.

Throughout this process, the superior executive will set up a warm, friendly, "I'm-really-trying-to-help" atmosphere. He will empathetically endeavor to seek information and allow the employee to unload completely.

After all this is completed, what do we do now? What is the best way to handle this situation? We weigh the facts and information given us by the employee. We may have come to a compromise. We may be able to move a complete solution in one direction. We may have to go through a trial basis with certain follow-up checks. There may be some changes necessary in job duties. One thing is certain: If the employee has allowed you to get close to him, and has communicated honestly, you must stay close during his rebuilding process. If he understands that you are sincerely and honestly trying to help him solve the problems, he will probably react dynamically.

If you wind up back in your busy schedule without time for consideration, concern, and periodic conversational follow-up, he may view your interest as superficial—something with which you are not as concerned as you said. There is another side, too. In thinking back over some of the cases I have been involved in, I remember one very clearly. After the process had gotten to the point of endeavoring to work out a new climate which would create challenge and bring back the spark, it ended abruptly. Because of the open and informal discussion which had taken place, the employee finally admitted he did not want to make the necessary effort to relight his flame. The ultimate conclusion came from his own mouth. "I think I had better look for another job." While that answer was not the one I had most wanted to hear, it was an honest one, which had been pondered greatly. Again, everybody benefited: We had achieved an honest dialogue and another human being had come face-to-face with himself.

We must take responsibility upon ourselves for the people we dare to direct. If we do not, we are allowing them to become everybody's responsibility, and everybody's responsibility is nobody's responsibility.

Another way to build strong employees is to break them of being yes-men and -women. I know you may think you are open, fair, easygoing, and all the rest, but they know who cracks the whip and who can hire and fire. Maybe it isn't you. Maybe it is one of your vice presidents or managers. Whoever it is in your organization, get it straight if you want the most from your people. They must feel that they do not have to agree with you. I have never learned anything new from anyone who merely agreed with me. Although often agreement gives us a better feeling or helps to solidify our understanding in connection with learning something new, it is of no help.

When you move into a position of authority, it is not good to have people who work for you or service or sell to you constantly agreeing with you. Yet it is almost certain to happen because you are the boss or the buyer. Exactly why is it not good? First, no one is totally right all the time. Second, it does not build the quality of person who can be proud and fulfilled in various positions. Third, the loss to one's company in productivity and doing the job in the best possible way is tremendous. They are all tied together. Rather than take them separately, let us examine them as they are intertwined.

HOW TO PERMIT PEOPLE TO FEEL FULFILLED

Many who are in positions of authority do not have a principle of good management which in essence says, "People who are allowed to be or feel personally fulfilled will outproduce, outprotect, outprofit, and in general outbuild all others." One of the ways a person becomes fulfilled in an on-the-job situation is to be sincerely listened to. Many managers say, "My door is always open to my people here." Sure, the door may be open physically, but is the mind really open? It is a great quality to be able to honestly listen and evaluate.

There is also a lot we all need to learn about the ability to not feel threatened or insecure when someone does not agree with us. Subordinates often agree with us because we are their boss, not because we are necessarily right or know the best way to accomplish the most desirable results.

How do you react when another questions the way you handled or propose to handle a situation or decision? Okay, so you do not try to defend your position as hard as you sued to. You have learned as you have matured. But do you sometimes slip and assume a defensive posture?

Why not try asking questions about others' ideas on the problem and really try to become an objective evaluator? Perhaps the combination of the ideas of others and your own will produce the best results. As an evaluator, you should not become a salesman defending your ideas. Sit quietly, listen, and ask questions. If you begin to expound first on your ideas, chances are the other person will quickly realize his subordinate position and agree with you for his own job security.

One of the tests of a great manager-leader is how well he can produce the best results. We all agree with that. Think about this: People who are on the daily firing line know a great deal about the problems and their possible solutions. If you want the benefit of knowing about the real problems and the possible solutions, become a warm, empathetic listener-evaluator. Help them decide the best course of action, turn them loose in that direction, and watch the smoke. People will pull out all the stops in an effort to make "their" idea work. Result: Your people will make your department and your company work. You are producing results; thus, you are also a success. Yes, I realize I'm back to Abraham Maslow again.

The next time you are about to say, "My door is always open," question yourself. Is it really? Why not make a commitment to stop giving so many orders or offering ideas first? We cannot learn anything new from people who always agree with us. And, after all, you are the boss. Become good at asking others for their ideas and sincerely listening.

HOW TO DECIDE BETWEEN RIGHT AND WRONG

A large part of working with people is the ability to decide between right and wrong. One of the qualifications of a good manager is teaching employees also to make that same type of decision. Some years ago, Dr. Harry Emerson Fosdick laid out six points to test oneself on just that subject. Here they are:

1. Does the course of action you plan to follow seem logical and reasonable? Never mind what anyone else has to say. Does it make sense to you? If it does, it is probably right.
2. Does it pass the test of sportsmanship? In other words, if everyone followed this same course of action, would the results be beneficial for all?
3. Where will your plan of action lead? How will it affect others? What will it do to you?
4. Will you think well of yourself when you look back at what you have done?
5. Try to separate yourself from the problem. Pretend for a moment it is the problem of the person you most admire. Ask yourself how that person would handle it.
6. Hold up the final decision to the glaring light of publicity. Would you want your family and friends to know what you have done? The decisions we make in the hope that no one will find out are usually wrong.

How well your individual men and women perform shows exactly how good you are as a leader. It's performance that counts. Like the immortal words of Mae West, "It's not how many men you have in your life that counts, it's how much life you have in your men."

37

What Will Be Your
Direction Now?

Would You Like to Learn How to Make Changes

A diamond is a chunk of coal that made good under pressure

I hope your personal direction, no matter what the pressure, will constantly be a direction of change. As fast as technology and society are pyramiding into change, it becomes necessary continually to modify. If you do not, you may achieve change but it will probably be at a much lower level than could be reached.

HOW TO APPROACH CHANGE

To learn how to change is a manager's first reaction toward change itself. In general, there are two basic ways to approach change and the question marks it usually produces. As in football, there are the offensive and the defensive ways.

The offensive way dictates that you set up a continual search for new ideas, opportunities, and danger signals which pending or actual change has brought to your professional world. By discovering and then making your changes quickly, you become a leader and thus bring about change in your company and industry. It may be that stitch in time that saves nine, or it may be seeing the new wave coming and positioning yourself so you can ride high by being "firstest with the mostest."

Then there is the defensive way. This sort of manager and company exist in the business world in spite of themselves. They go along with the wave. They recognize it only because their boat begins to rock. "Oh, there is a big wave. We had better put on our life jackets and hold on. Give the engine a little more gas so we can ride it out better." They are after-the-fact, passive adjusters to change.

Remember that to write the word *crisis* in Chinese, the Orientals combine the Chinese characters for the words *opportunity* and *danger*. Change can be viewed in the same way. It can be an opportunity or a threat. Great leaders succeed as innovators of change. Even those who are not creative as leaders of change do far better if they view it, when it comes, as opportunity. Management cannot just say they will seek out change and be aware. It requires creative talent with the free enterprise type of entrepreneurial desires. You must seek out this type of talent in your organization or hire it. I do not say it is impossible to teach. I say it is tough and in order to teach it, top management must have it to start with.

The doctrine of change says, "I accept the fact we do not have to keep on doing things the same old way just because we have always done them that way." Remember, when you are examining your methods, effectiveness and efficiency are not the same. You are efficient by doing things right. You are effective by doing the right things. There is a big difference. It is useless to do things with great efficiency which need not have been done at all.

Each effort your organization puts forth and every decision you make should be done over with the cross-examination skill of a good prosecuting attorney. Get rid of extra baggage; cut unnecessary steps; gear to meet the marketplace of change. Encourage every employee to utilize every ounce of ability they have when the opportunity of creative change presents itself. Decide where your money and manpower can make the biggest impact and address all efforts accordingly.

As I have reread these many pages, I am aware that there is so much more to be said on this huge subject of franchising and building a business. Perhaps I should have begun this book with the word "and..." because there has been so much that has gone on before this. No experience ever really begins. There was always something that preceded it. Perhaps what really began was our additional awareness of something going on.

Likewise, I should end with the word "and..." because there is so much more to come after this book. No story ever ends. Something more will happen. This is true for franchising more than most other business methods.

Perhaps it might be said we live in a world of etcetera, etcetera, etcetera, since there is always more to start with than we can take into account; always more to say than we possibly can; always more to end with than we can imagine. So for my parting assist, please remember, this is a must for every franchisor: *and*...

38

Government Financial and Management Assistance Programs

171 Names and Addresses to Help You

*It's nice to have a little help from
a friend.*

MINORITY BUSINESS DEVELOPMENT AGENCY

The Minority Business Development Agency (MBDA) was established within the Department of Commerce to be the focal point of the federal government's efforts to assist the establishment of new minority enterprises and the expansion of existing ones.

MBDA is responsible for coordinating operations of the federal government which may contribute to establishing and strengthening minority enterprise. It promotes and mobilizes the activities and resources of state and local governments, businesses, and other private groups and organizations to further minority business growth; and coordinates such programs of the federal agencies. The office also maintains a center for the collection, analysis, and dissemination of information to assist the establishment and operation of minority businesses.

To provide local assistance to prospective and existing minority business persons, MBDA operates six regional and twelve field offices. It has also affiliated with business development organizations in cities with substantial minority populations. If you operate a minority business enterprise and are in need of assistance, or represent a potential new business enterprise, contact an MBDA regional or district office for further assistance:

Atlanta Regional Office

Atlanta Region

MBDA Regional Director
1371 Peachtree St., NW, Suite 505
Atlanta, GA 30309
(404) 881–4091

MBDA District Officer
908 20th St., Room 215
Birmingham, AL 35205
(205) 254–0698

MBDA District Officer
1371 Peachtree St., NE, Suite 505
Atlanta, GA 30309
(404) 881–7609

MBDA District Officer
216 Federal Bldg.
Miami, FL 33130
(305) 350–5054

MBDA District Officer
747 Kefauver Federal Bldg.
Nashville, TN 37203

Chicago Regional Office

Chicago Region

MBDA Regional Director
55 E. Monroe St., Room 1440
Chicago, IL 60603
(312) 353–0182

MBDA District Officer
3130 Troost Ave.
Kansas City, MO 64109
(816) 374–3381

MBDA District Officer
535 Federal Courthouse Bldg.
Detroit, MI 48226
(313) 226–4835

MBDA District Officer
666 Euclid Ave., Room 600
Cleveland, OH 44114
(216) 522–5404

MBDA District Officer
1114 Market St., Room 633
St. Louis, MO 63101
(314) 425–6426

MBDA District Officer
108 Federal Courts Bldg.
Minneapolis, MN 55401
(612) 725–2044

Dallas Regional Office

Dallas Region

MBDA Regional Director
1100 Commerce St., Room 7819
Dallas, TX 75242
(214) 729–8001

MBDA District Officer
909 17th St., Room 509
Denver, CO 80202
(303) 837–2767

MBDA District Officer
Marquette, NW, Room 1001
Albuquerque, NM 87101
(505) 766–3379

MBDA District Officer
South Street, Room 616
New Orleans, LA 70130
(504) 389–2935

MBDA District Officer
B412 Federal Bldg.
San Antonio, TX 78206
(512) 229–5511

MBDA District Officer
600 W. Capitol Ave., Room 234
Little Rock, AR 72201
(501) 378–6169

MBDA District Officer
2525 Murworth, Suite 105
Houston, TX 77054
(713) 226–5732

New York Regional Office

New York Region

MBDA Acting Regional Director
26 Federal Plaza, Suite 36116
New York, NY 10007
(212) 264–3262

MBDA District Officer
26 Federal Plaza, 36th Floor
New York, NY 10278
(212) 264–4382

MBDA District Officer
441 Stuart St., Seventh Floor
Boston, MA 02116
(617) 223–3726

MBDA District Officer
1111 W. Huron St., Room 500
Buffalo, NY 14202
(716) 846–4387

MBDA District Officer
970 Broad St., Room 1653
Newark, NJ 07102
(201) 645–6497

San Francisco Regional Office

San Francisco Region

MBDA Regional Director
15045 Federal Bldg.
San Francisco, CA 94102
(415) 556-7234

MBDA District Officer
15043 Federal Bldg., Room 15045
San Francisco, CA 94102
(415) 556-6065

MBDA District Officer
2500 Wilshire Blvd., Room 908
Los Angeles, CA 90057
(213) 688-7157

MBDA District Officer
3206 Federal Bldg.
Seattle, WA 98174
(206) 442-2437

MBDA District Officer
511 N.W. Broadway, Room 647
Portland, OR 97209
(503) 423-4997

MBDA District Officer
2940 Valley Bank Center
Phoenix, AZ 85073
(602) 261-3502

MBDA District Officer
P.O. Box 50189
Honolulu, HI 96850
(808) 546-3796

Washington Regional Office

Washington Regional

MBDA Regional Director
1730 K St., NW, Room 420
Washington, DC 20006
(202) 634-7897

MBDA District Officer
Fallon Federal Bldg., Box 286
Baltimore, MD 21201
(301) 962-3231

MBDA District Officer
US Dept. of Commerce, Room
5628
Washington, DC 20230
(202) 377-5098

MBDA District Officer
Room 7010, Federal Bldg.
Richmond, VA 23240
(804) 771-2050

MBDA District Officer
W. J. Creen Federal Bldg.
600 Arch St., Room 9436
Philadelphia, PA 19106
(215) 597–9236

MBDA District Officer
614 Federal Bldg.
Pittsburgh, PA 15222
(412) 644–5882

U.S. DEPARTMENT OF COMMERCE

International Trade Administration

Alabama

Suite 200–201
908 South 20th St.
Birmingham, AL 35205
(205) 254–1331

Alaska

701 C St.
P.O. Box 32
Anchorage, AK 99513
(907) 271–5041

Arizona

Suite 2950 Valley Bank Center
201 North Central Avenue
Phoenix, AZ 85004
(602) 261–3285

Arkansas

Suite 635, Savers Federal Bldg.
320 W. Capitol Ave.
Little Rock, AR 72201
(501) 387–5794

California

Room 800, 11777 San Vincente
   Blvd.
Los Angeles, CA 90049
(213) 824–7591

Federal Bldg., Box 36013
450 Golden Gate Avenue
San Francisco, CA 94102
(415) 556–5860

Colorado

Room 165, New Customhouse
19th & Stout St.
Denver, CO 88202
(303) 837–3246

Connecticut

Room 610-B Federal Office Bldg.
450 Main St.
Hartford, CT 06103
(203) 244–3530

Florida

Room 821, City Nat'l Bank Bldg.
25 West Flagler St.
Miami, FL 33130
(305) 350–5267

Georgia

Suite 600, 1365 Peachtree St., NE
Atlanta, GA 30309
(404) 881–7000

222 U.S. Courthouse & P.O. Bldg.
125–29 Bull St.
Savannah, GA 31402
(912) 944–4204

Hawaii

4106 Federal Bldg.
300 Ala Moana Blvd.
Honolulu, HI 96850
(808) 546–8694

Illinois

1406 Mid Continental Plaza Bldg.
55 East Monroe St.
Chicago, IL 60603
(312) 353–4450

Indiana

357 U.S. Courthouse & Federal
  Office Bldg.
46 East Ohio St.
Indianapolis, IN 46204
(317) 269–6214

Iowa

817 Federal Bldg.
210 Walnut St.
Des Moines, IA 50309
(515) 284–4222

Kentucky

Room 636, U.S. P.O. Bldg.
and Court House Bldg.
Louisville, KY 40202
(502) 582–5066

Louisiana

432 International Trade Mart
No. 2 Canal St.
New Orleans, LA 70130
(504) 589–6546

Maryland

415 U.S. Customhouse
Gay and Lombard Streets
Baltimore, MD 21202
(301) 962–3560

Massachusetts

10th Floor
441 Stuart St.
Boston, MA 20116
(617) 223–2312

Michigan

445 Federal Bldg.
231 W. Lafayette
Detroit, MI 48226
(313) 226–3650

Minnesota

218 Federal Bldg.
110 S. Fourth St.
Minneapolis, MN 55401
(612) 725–2133

Mississippi

City Center Plaza, Suite 550
200 Pascagoula
Jackson, MS 39201
(601) 969–4388

Missouri

120 S. Central Ave.
St. Louis, MO 63105
(314) 425-3302-4

Room 1840, 601 E. 12th St.
Kansas City, MO 64106
(816) 374-3142

Nebraska

300 S. 19th St.
Omaha, NE 68102
(402) 221-3664

Nevada

2028 Federal Bldg.
300 Booth St.
Reno, NV 89509
(702) 784-5203

New Jersey

4th Floor, Gateway Bldg.
Market St. & Penn Plaza
Newark, NJ 07102
(201) 645-6214

New Mexico

505 Marquette Ave. NW
Suite 1015
Albuquerque, NM 87102
(505) 766-2386

New York

1312 Federal Bldg.
111 West Huron St.
Buffalo, NY 14202
(716) 846-4191

37th Floor, Federal Office Bldg.
26 Federal Plaza, Foley Sq.
New York, NY 10007
(212) 264-0634

North Carolina

203 Federal Bldg.
West Market St., P.O. Box 1950
Greensboro, NC 27402
(919) 378-5345

Ohio

10504 Federal Office Bldg.
550 Main St.
Cincinnati, OH 45202
(513) 684-2944

Room 600, 666 Euclid Ave.
Cleveland, OH 44114
(216) 522-4750

Oregon

Room 618, 1220 SW 3rd Ave.
Portland, OR 97204
(504) 221-3001

Pennsylvania

9448 Federal Bldg.
600 Arch St.
Philadelphia, PA 19106
(215) 597-2866

2002 Federal Bldg.
1000 Liberty Ave.
Pittsburgh, PA 15222
(412) 644-2850

Puerto Rico

Room 659, Federal Bldg.
San Juan, PR 00918
(809) 753–4555

South Carolina

1835 Assembly St.
Columbia, SC 29201
(803) 765–5345

Tennessee

Room 710
147 Jefferson Ave.
Memphis, TN 38103
(901) 521–3213

Texas

Room 7A5, 1100 Commerce St.
Dallas, TX 75242
(214) 767–0542

2625 Federal Bldg., Courthouse
515 Rusk St.
Houston, TX
(713) 226–4231

Utah

350 S. Main St.
Salt Lake City, UT 84101
(803) 524–5116

Virginia

8010 Federal Bldg.
400 North 8th St.
Richmond, VA 23240
(804) 771–2246

Washington

Room 706, Lake Union Bldg.
1700 Westlake Ave., North
Seattle, WA 98109
(206) 442–5615

West Virginia

3000 New Federal Bldg.
500 Quarrier St.
Charleston, WV 25301
(304) 343–6181, ext. 375

Wisconsin

Federal Bldg./U.S. Courthouse
517 East Wisconsin Ave.
Milwaukee, WI 53202
(414) 291–3473

Wyoming

6022 O'Mahoney Federal Center
2120 Capital Ave.
Cheyenne, WY
(307) 778–2220, ext. 2151

SMALL BUSINESS ADMINISTRATION

The Small Business Administration aids those planning to enter business as well as those in business. This assistance includes counseling and possible financial aid.

Counseling may be by SBA specialists or retired executives under the Service Corps of Retired Executives (SCORE) program, and could include various seminars or a combination of services, including reference publications.

Financial assistance may take the form of loans or the participation in, or guaranty of, loans made by financial institutions. Such assistance can be given only to those eligible applicants who are unable to provide the money from their own resources and who cannot obtain it on reasonable terms from banks, franchisors, or other usual business sources.

A list of Small Business Administration field offices follows, where more detailed information regarding the various services available can be obtained.

Regional Offices

Region 1 (Connecticut, Maine, Massachusetts, New Hampshire, Rhode Island, Vermont)
60 Batterymarch St.
Boston, MA 02110
(617) 223-3204

Region 2 (New Jersey, New York, Puerto Rico, Virgin Islands)
26 Federal Plaza, Room 29-118
New York, NY 10007
(212) 264-7772

Region 3 (Delaware, District of Columbia, Maryland, Pennsylvania, Virginia, W. Virginia)
231 S. Asaphs Rd.
Bala Cynwyd, PA 19004
(215) 569-5984

Region 4 (Alabama, Florida, Georgia, Kentucky, Mississippi, North Carolina, South Carolina, Tennessee)
1375 Peachtree St., NE
Atlanta, GA 30367
(404) 881-4963

Region 5 (Illinois, Indiana, Michigan, Minnesota, Ohio, Wisconsin)
Federal Bldg.
219 South Dearborn St., Room 838
Chicago, IL 60604
(312) 353-0355

Region 6 (Arkansas, Louisiana, New Mexico, Oklahoma, Texas)
1720 Regal Row
Regal Park Office Bldg.
Dallas, TX 75235
(214) 767-7643

Region 7 (Iowa, Kansas, Missouri, Nebraska)
911 Walnut St., 23rd Floor
Kansas City, MO 64106
(816) 374-5288

Region 8 (Colorado, Montana, North Dakota, South Dakota, Utah, Wyoming)
1405 Curtis St.
Denver, CO 80202
(303) 837-5763

Region 9 (Arizona, California, Hawaii, Nevada, Pacific Islands)
Federal Bldg.
450 Golden Gate Ave.
San Francisco, CA 94102
(415) 556-7487

Region 10 (Alaska, Idaho, Oregon, Washington)
710 2nd Ave., 5th Floor
Dexter Horton Bldg
Seattle, WA 98104
(206) 442-5676

District Offices

Region 1

150 Causeway St., Boston MA 02114 (617) 223-3224
302 High St., Holyoke, MA 01040 (413) 536-8770
Federal Bldg., 40 Western Ave., Room 512, Augusta, ME 04330
(207) 622-6171
55 Pleasant St., Rm. 211, Concord, NH 03301 (603) 224-4041
One Financial Plaza, Hartford, CT 06103 (203) 244-3600

Federal Bldg., 87 State St., Rm. 210, Montpelier, VT 05602
(802) 229–0538

40 Fountain St., Providence, RI 02903 (401) 528–4580

Region 2

Carlos Chardon Ave., Hato Rey, PR 00919 (809) 753–4572

970 Broad St., Rm. 1635, Newark, NJ 07102 (201) 645–2434

100 State St., Room 601, Rochester, NY 14614 (716) 263–6700

Federal Bldg., Room 1071, 100 South Clinton St., Syracuse, NY
13202 (315) 423–5383

111 West Huron St., Room 1311, Federal Bldg., Buffalo, NY 14202
(716) 846–4301

180 Clemens Ctr. Pkwy., Elmira, NY 14904 (607) 733–4686

445 Broadway, Albany, NY 12207 (518) 472–6300

Region 3

109 N. 3rd St., Room 301, Lowndes Bldg., Clarksburg, WV 26301
(304) 623–5361

Federal Bldg., 1000 Liberty Ave., Room 1401, Pittsburgh, PA
15222 (412) 644–2780

Federal Bldg., 400 North 8th St., Room 3015, Richmond, VA
23240 (804) 771–2617

1030 15th St., NW, 2nd Floor, Washington, DC 20417
(202) 653–6963

100 Chestnut St., Harrisburg, PA 17101 (717) 782–3840

20 N. Pennsylvania Ave., Wilkes-Barre, PA 18702 (717) 826–6497

844 King St., Federal Bldg., Room 5207, Wilmington, DE 19801
(302) 573–6294

8600 LaSalle Rd., Towson, MD 21204 (301) 962–4392

Region 4

908 South 20th St., Room 202, Birmingham, AL 35205 (205)
254–1344

230 S. Tryon St., Addison Bldg., Charlotte, NC 29202 (704)
371–6563

1835 Assembly St., Columbia, SC 29202 (803) 765–5376

100 West Capital St., Jackson, MS 30201 (601) 960–9378

Federal Bldg., 400 West Bay St., Room 261, Jacksonville, FL
32202 (904) 691–3792

2222 Ponce de Leon Blvd., 5th Floor, Miami, FL 33184
(305) 350–5521

404 James Robertson Pkwy., Nashville, TN 37219 (615) 251–5881

502 South Gay St., Room 307, Fidelity Bankers Bldg., Knoxville,
TN 37902 (615) 637–9300

215 South Evans St., Greenville, NC 27834 (919) 752–3798

111 Fred Haise Blvd., Gulf National Life Ins. Bldg., 2nd Floor,
Biloxi, MS (601) 435–3676

700 Twiggs St., Suite 607, Tampa, FL 33602 (813) 228–2594

Federal Bldg., 167 N. Main St., Room 211, Memphis, TN 38103
(901) 521–3588

Region 5

Four North Old State Plaza, Springfield, IL 62702 (217) 955–4200

1240 East 9th St., Room 317, Cleveland, OH 44199 (216) 522–4194

85 Marconi Blvd., Columbus, OH 43215 (614) 469–6860

Federal Bldg., 550 Main St., Cincinnati, OH 45202 (513) 684–2814

477 Michigan Ave., McNamara Bldg., Detroit, MI 48226 (313)
226–7241

575 N. Pennsylvania Ave., Century Bldg., Indianapolis, IN 46204
(317) 331–7000

212 East Washington Ave., Room 552, Madison, WI 53703
(608) 264–5205

100 North 6th St., Minneapolis, MN 55403 (612) 725–2358

540 W. Kaye Ave., Marquette, MI 49855 (906) 225–1108

Federal Bldg., 517 East Wisconsin Ave., Room 246, Milwaukee,
WI 53202 (414) 291–3941

500 S. Barstow St., Room 16, Federal Office Bldg., & U.S.
Courthouse, Eau Claire, WI 54701 (715) 834–9012

Region 6

5000 Marble Ave., NE, Patio Plaza Bldg., Albuquerque, NM 87110
(505) 766–3430

One Allen Center, 500 Dallas, Houston, TX 77002 (713) 226–4341

320 West Capitol Ave., Little Rock, AR 72201 (501) 378–5871

1205 Texas Ave., Lubbock, TX 79408 (806) 762–7466

222 East Van Buren St., Harlingen, TX 78550 (Lower Rio Grande Valley) (512) 423–8934

1000 South Washington St., Marshall, TX 75670 (214) 935–5257

Plaza Tower, 17th Floor, 1011 Howard Ave., New Orleans, LA 70113 (504) 589–6685

200 NW 5th St., Suite 670, Oklahoma City, OK 73102 (405) 231–4301

727 E. Durango, Room A–513, San Antonio, TX 78206 (512) 229–6250

1100 Commerce St., Dallas, TX 75202 (214) 767–0605

4100 Rio Bravo, Suite 300, El Paso, TX 79902 (915) 543–7586

3105 Leopard St., Corpus Christi, TX 78408 (512) 888–3331

Region 7

New Federal Bldg., 210 Walnut St., Room 749, Des Moines, IA 50309 (515) 284–4422

19th and Farnam Sts., Empire State Bldg., Omaha, NE 68102 (402) 221–4691

Suite 2500, Mercantile Tower, St. Louis, MO 63101 (314) 425–4191

110 East Waterman, Wichita, KS 67202 (316) 267–6511

Region 8

Room 4001, Federal Bldg., 100 East B St., Casper, WY 82601 (307) 265–5266

301 S. Park, Room 528, Helena, MT 59601 (406) 449–5381

Federal Bldg., 657 2nd Ave. N., Room 218, Fargo, ND 58102 (701) 237–5771

Federal Bldg., 125 South State St., Room 2237, Salt Lake City, UT 84111 (801) 425–5800

101 South Main Ave., Sioux Falls, SD 57102 (605) 336–2980

515 9th Street, Federal Bldg., Rapid City, SD 57701 (605) 343–5074

Region 9

300 Ala Moana Blvd., Honolulu, HI 96850 (808) 546–8950

350 S. Figueroa St., Los Angeles, CA 90071 (213) 688–2956

3030 North Central Ave., Phoenix, AZ 85012 (602) 241–2200

880 Front St., San Diego, CA 92101 (714) 293–5440

301 E. Stewart, Las Vegas, NV 89121 (702) 385–6611

1229 N. St., Fresno, CA 93721 (209) 487–5189

Region 10

1016 West 6th Ave., Suite 200, Anchorage Legal Center,
Anchorage, AK 99501 (907) 271–4022

101 12th Ave., Fairbanks, AK 99701 (907) 452–1951

1005 Main St., Boise, ID 83701 (208) 334–2200

1220 SW Third Ave., Portland, OR 97205 (503) 221–2682

Court House Bldg., Room 651, Spokane, WA 99210 (509) 456–5310

INTERNAL REVENUE SERVICE, DEPARTMENT OF THE TREASURY

The Internal Revenue Service offers a number of services to assist new business executives in understanding and meeting their federal tax obligations. For example, a *Mr. Businessman's Kit* (Publication 454), which contains informational publications, forms, instructions, and samples of notices that the IRS issues to business concerns, is available free.

This kit is a convenient place to store retained copies of tax returns and employee information. It also contains a checklist of tax returns and a tax calendar of due dates for filing returns and paying taxes identified on the folder. Copies of the kit may be obtained from local offices of the Internal Revenue Service. Employees of the IRS are available to explain items in the kit and answer questions about the tax forms; how to complete them; requirements for withholding, depositing, reporting federal income and social security taxes; and the federal unemployment tax. Copies of the kit may also be obtained by writing to the district director, who will have it delivered and explained at a mutually convenient time.

The *Tax Guide for Small Business* (Publication 334) may also be obtained free from local offices of the IRS, the district director, of the Superintendent of Documents, U.S. Government Printing Office, Washington, DE 20402.

Glossary

*I'll always have a good word for you,
my friend.*

The definitions herein are generally explained specifically as the word(s) relates to the franchise system.

AREA FRANCHISE. *See* MASTER FRANCHISE.

COPYRIGHT. The right of a person to use, and license others to use, an intellectual property such as a book, pamphlet, advertising copy, or other published material.

DISCLOSURE DOCUMENTS. Documents which reveal facts to others. These facts may be helpful or harmful to the franchisor, such as disclosing poor service, credit, etc. *See* UFOC.

DISTRIBUTORSHIP. A right granted by a manufacturer or wholesaler to sell his product to others. A distributorship is generally not considered a franchise.

FEASIBILITY STUDY. A study usually made by an independent party qualified to do such work. A study which considers factors in the marketplace and gives conclusions as to whether or not a service or product can be undertaken profitably.

FRANCHISE. An agreement, for consideration, by which a person permits the distribution of goods or services under his trademark, service mark, or trade name, during which time the franchisor retains control over others or renders significant assistance to others. (This definition is basically the one used by the Federal Trade Commission.)

FRANCHISE FEE. Any fee paid by a franchisee to the franchisor for the franchise. Usually this is a flat fee paid initially, as distinguished from a royalty fee.

FRANCHISOR. A person or company issuing or granting a franchise or license to a franchisee or licensee.

FRANCHISEE. A person or company to whom the right (franchise or license) to conduct a business is granted by the franchisor or licensor.

IDENTIFYING ITEMS. Those items (such as paper products, uniforms, ashtrays, or signs) usually required to be used in a franchisee's business, which display the marks of the franchisor.

LICENSE. *See* FRANCHISE.

MANUALS. Comprehensive guidelines advising a franchisee how to operate the franchised business. They cover various aspects of the business, including business procedures. Usually there are several manuals such as accounting, personnel, advertising, operations, marketing, maintenance, sales, furnishings, and training.

MASTER FRANCHISE. A franchise granted for the development of a specific area—that is, a region, territory, area, country, or other specific geographically defined area. It usually carries with it the right to subfranchise others.

PRO FORMA. A balance sheet and profit and loss statement which assumes levels of revenue and expense, capital assets, liabilities, and net worth. They should be based on existing historical operation results. Generally they are included in a feasibility study and may come from the franchisor.

QUALITY CONTROL. The checks by which the franchisor enforces the rules of operation, product and service quality. They are usually also listed in the manuals. Quality control implies that inspectors will visit each franchisee and check the operation of the franchised outlet.

REGIONAL FRANCHISE. *See* MASTER FRANCHISE.

REGISTRATION. A requirement in several states that specific information be submitted and approved by those regulatory authorities before franchises may be offered for sale. Material in the registration is more extensive than that in disclosure documents. The Federal Trade Commission (FTC) has no provision for registration, thus the franchisor need only prepare an accurate and complete disclosure document according to the regulations.

ROBINSON-PATMAN ACT. One of the group of antitrust laws; a federal law to prevent price discrimination in interstate commerce concerning franchising. It deals with the area of price fixing, where the franchisor imposes product prices on the end user, or where one or more franchisees agree on a price or prices for products or services.

Reduction of prices for the purpose of harming competition is also a violation of the act.

ROYALTY FEE. An ongoing fee paid by the franchisee to the franchisor, usually in the form of a percentage of gross sales.

SERVICE MARK. A mark used in the sale or advertising of services to identify the services of one person and distinguish them from the services of others. The word *trademark* is specifically associated with goods or products such as automobiles, whereas service marks relate to employment agencies, real estate chains, and the like. They are both afforded the same protection under the law.

SHERMAN ANTITRUST ACT. One of the group of antitrust laws providing, in general, that it is illegal to conspire to restrain trade. Franchisee associations must be carefully monitored and franchise agreements drafted (there are certain case law exceptions) to avoid allocation of territories or fixing prices. As it affects franchising, the Sherman Act is applied to activities, whereas the Robinson-Patman Act can only apply to matters involved in two or more states. Each body of law has been enlarged and modified by subsequent acts. There are other antitrust acts, notably the Federal Trade Commission Act, the Clayton Act, the state antitrust laws, and "Little" FTC acts.

SUBFRANCHISE. A franchise right granted to a franchisee to further franchise others to operate under the franchisor's system. The intermediate franchisee is often referred to as the *master franchisee*. Various responsibilities to the subfranchisee may be divided between the franchisor and master franchisee.

TERRITORIAL FRANCHISE. *See* MASTER FRANCHISE.

TRADEMARK OR MARK. A trademark is a symbol used to identify the commercial operations of a company (may be the company name). A name or symbol may be used to identify one or more products and may be used in combination with the company's other trademarks or trade names. Franchises usually provide for the franchisee to use the marks of the franchisor and the name associated with a product. Before federal registration, the symbol *TM* or *SM* may be affixed near the words making up the mark or symbol to inform the public it is intended that the name be protected. After federal registration of the mark, the symbol *R* is used.

UNIFORM OFFERING CIRCULAR (UFOC). A disclosure document containing required information supplied by the franchisor to the franchisee. *See* DISCLOSURE DOCUMENT.

The world of franchising is like a beautiful, mysterious, ever-changing, ever-intriguing woman. It can absorb you, drive you wild, keep you up late at night, be divinely rewarding, give you ulcers, and turn you gray. I love the franchising concept of marketing a business.

In this industry, one can possibly die from confusion, but never from boredom. There is always something new happening—new products, new techniques, new marketing concepts, new economic conditions to contend with, or new laws and regulations that require 225 pounds of additional paperwork each year.

When establishing or expanding the franchising method of distribution for your product or service, it is critically important to know what questions to ask. In fact, I have found that answering is not nearly as difficult when you know the questions.

Imagine trying to solve a problem in a business that you know very little about. It undoubtedly becomes a tough situation. Possibly this is the way one might feel about considering franchising if one has little or no experience in the field.

Experience not only gives the answers, it also allows one to know some of the questions. In this also lies some danger. The saying, "a little knowledge is dangerous," was never more true than in connection with franchising.

Index

A

Accounting Department, 148–153
  computers, 152–53
Advertising agency, 158–59
  working with, 160–62
  ground rules, 160–62
Advertising, free, 125–27
Architecture and design, 113–115
  changing, 114–115
Area franchises, (See Distributorships)

B

Board of Directors:
  description, 33
  guidelines, 36–38
  salary, 36
  selection, 34
  training, 34–36
Brainstorming, 193–194
Budget, establishing, 149–50
Building design, 113
Burnout, (See Employee burnout)
Business:
  experience, 26–27
  failure, 26–31
  going public, 80
  record keeping, 28
  selling out, 80–81
  single-line sales, 28–29
  starting capital, 27–28
  syndicate, 79
"Business format franchising," 2

C

Change:
  approaching, 204
  defensive, 205
  offensive, 204
  opportunity or threat, 205
Code of Citizenship, 50
Communication, 105
  elements, 105–106
  feedback, 112
  "Quick Draw McGraw" technique, 107
  teaching employees, 107–108
  telephone, telegram, mailgram, 184–85
  writing and speaking, 110-12
Company-owned operations, 21–22
  advantages, 21
Computers and manpower, 152–53
Consultants:
  choosing, 61–64
  definition, 59
  fees, 64–65
  what they do, 60–61
Contingent fee, 65
Creativity, a valuable tool, 159

D

Demographics, 54
Departments, setting up, 169–70
Designing your operation, 17
Distributorships, 23

E

Employee burnout, 197–98
Employee burnout, preventive measures, 196
Executive qualifications, 187–190

Expansion:
  capital, 20–21
  company owned vs. franchised units, 20–25
  items to consider, 171–72

F

Failure, thirty reasons for, 30–31
Federal Trade Commission (FTC), 67
Fees:
  accounting for, 89
  establishing, 88
Field Inspector, 144–46
Financial assistance, 148
Fixed amount contract, 65
Fluid drive, 189
Foreign Franchise Associations, 179
Foreign growth, statistics, 177–78
Foreign markets, 177
Franchise:
  definition, 2
  elements, 18
  evaluating, 55
  keep or sell, 7
  location, 129–30
  president, 33
  qualifying your business, 6
  sales, 116–17
  small companies, 176
  traditional, 2
Franchise Agreement, 82–87
  goals, 82–83
  items to consider, 84–87
Franchise contract:
  changing contracts, 50–51
  implied contract of human relations, 49–52
  legal contract, 49–50
Franchise laws, regulations, and rulings, 69
Franchise laws, states with, 69–76
Franchise legal specialist, 84
Franchisee:
  potential, 123–24
  psychological profile, 93
  what they look for, 56–57
Franchisee Association, 98
  bylaws, 100–101
  dos and don'ts, 102–103
  franchisor participation, 101–102
Franchisees:
  communication, 98
  "human qualifications," 91
  selecting, 91–94, 141–42
Franchise-owned operations, 22
  advantages, 22
Franchisees, why do franchisees buy? 9
Franchising:
  designing your operation, 16
  distributorships, 23
  establishing fees, 88
  the future, 12
  trends and predictions, 13
  why go into? 7
Franchising company's life, 18–19
Franchisor-franchisee relations, 95
FTC franchising rule, 67–68

G

Government financial programs, 207–225

H

Hybrid franchises, 3

I

Internal Revenue Service, 225
    Department of the Treasury, 225
    Mr. Businessman's Kit, 225
International Franchise Association (IFA), 5, 67, 77-78
    Code of Ethics, 78
    membership, 78
International markets, 174-75
International markets, rules for success, 175-76
Interviews, 165-68
    cardinal rules, 167-68
    image, 166
    preparation, 165-66

L

Laws and regulations, 66-76
Lawyers, selecting, 66-67
Legislative Affairs Department, 181
Legislative assistance, 180
Legislators:
    communication tools, 182
    communication with, 182
    contacts with, 183-84
    importance of, 180-85
    working with, 181-82
Locations:
    using computers, 130-32
    selecting, 130-32
Long-range planning (LR), 39-48
    benefits, 42
    picking your team, 41-42
    who should guide you? 45-46

M

McDonald's, 17, 28
Management Assistance Programs, 207-225
Management techniques, 192-93
    psychology, 192-93
    results of, 194-197
Management training, 34-36
Marketing, company image, 163-165
    eliminating sales, 157-58
    free, 155
Marketing Department, 154-168
Marketing plan, elements of, 162-63
Master franchises, 90
Minority Business Development Agency (MBDA), 207-208

N

"Need," (for franchise), 15

O

Operations Department, 143-47
Operations Manual, 144

P

People:
    burnout, 197
    deciding right or wrong, 203
    different ideas, 198-199
    fulfillment, 202-203
    working with, 191-203
Per diem, 65
Planning process, critical steps, 42-45
Planning team, 41-42
"Psychic remuneration," 97
Public relations, 125
Public relations, guide to, 156-57

Q

Quality control, 146-47

R

Real estate brokers, 132-34
Real estate brokers, selecting, 134-36
"Realistic Creativity," 16
Regional franchise, 23
Regional franchise, selecting, 23-25
Regional franchisees, 23-25
Retainer, 65
Return on assets (ROA), 27
Return on equity (ROE), 27
Royalty fee, 88

S

Sales, 116
    leads, 124-25
    salesperson's needs, 122-23
    territories, 120-21
    tools, 117-19
S-D-R (Send-Decode-Reaction), 105-106, 110
Selling creativity, 16
Short-range planning, 39
Site Approval Committee, 128-29
Speeches, 165-68
Speeches, preparation, 166
Subfranchising, 172-73
Subfranchising, problems with, 172
Successful people, choosing, 186-87

T

Tax Guide for Small Business, 255
Traditional franchise, 2
Training Department:
    investing in, 137
    purpose, 140
    starting off, 138-39
Technical language, 106
Twenty-First Century Management Techniques, 192, 195

U

Uniform Franchise Offering Circular (UFOC), 67

W

World Council of Franchise Associations, 176